NO OTHER GOD

A PRACTICAL LOOK AT A PERSONAL GOD

TRANSLATED WORKS OF PIERRE VIRET

The Catechism of Pierre Viret

The Christian and the Magistrate

His Glorious Bride

Jesus Christ, the Believer's Comfort and Joy

Letters of Comfort to the Persecuted Church

Marvelous Trinity

Simple Exposition of the Christian Faith

Pierre Viret: the Angel of the Reformation

VIRET DECALOGUE COMMENTARY SERIES

No Other God

Nothing Like God

Taking His Name in Vain

Remember the Sabbath Day

Honor thy Father and Mother

Thou Shalt Not Kill: A Plea for Life

Thou Shalt Not Commit Adultery

Thou Shalt Not Steal

Defend the Truth

Thou Shalt Not Covet

NO OTHER
GOD

A PRACTICAL LOOK AT A
PERSONAL GOD

by Pierre Viret

with a sermon by John Calvin

Translated by R. A. Sheats

Psalm 78 Ministries

www.psalm78ministries.com

No Other God: A Practical Look at a Personal God

by Pierre Viret, with a sermon by John Calvin

Translated by R. A. Sheats

Second edition

Published by:

Psalm 78 Ministries
P. O. Box 950
Monticello, FL 32345

www.psalm78ministries.com

Biblical quotations are taken from the King James Version of the Holy Scriptures. Divine pronouns have been capitalized.

TABLE OF CONTENTS

Translator's Note

No Other God: A Practical Look at a Personal God is an English translation of the first two chapters of Viret's commentary on the Ten Commandments, published originally in 1554 in French under the title *Exposition familiere sur les Dix Commandemens de la Loy* and printed in Geneva. It later appeared in an enlarged 1564 edition under the title *Instruction Chrestienne en la doctrine de la loy et de l'Evangile.* The text for this English translation has been taken from the 1564 French edition.

With the intention of presenting his readers with an easily-understood, down-to-earth exposition of the Ten Commandments, Viret wrote his commentary as a conversation between two fictitious characters, Daniel and Timothy. Within *No Other God,* Timothy and Daniel discuss the preface to the Law as well as the first commandment.

When originally published, Viret's commentary included an introduction that explained the necessity of a Law provided to mankind by an all-wise, sovereign God. This introduction has not been included in this book because it has been published separately in a book entitled *The Christian and the Magistrate* (Psalm 78 Ministries, 2015), in which it appears as the first chapter of that work.

Scripture quotations are taken from the King James Version of the Holy Bible. Where Viret cites Scripture but does not quote verbatim, his wording has been retained and the Scriptural reference placed in parentheses. Viret's work has been abridged and chapter breaks and titles have been added for ease of comprehension and do not appear in the original French.

A year after Viret's work on the Ten Commandments

came to print, John Calvin began preaching through the book of Deuteronomy to his congregation in Geneva. The text which forms the final chapter of this book is taken from his sermon on Deuteronomy 5:4-7, translated from the published version *Sermons de M. Jean Calvin sur le v. livre de Moyse nommé Deuteronome* (Thomas Courteau, Geneva, 1567).

ONE

God's Preface to His Law

"I am the Lord thy God,
which have brought thee out of the land of Egypt,
out of the house of bondage."

— Exodus 20:1

GOD'S PREFACE TO HIS LAW AND THE TITLES HE GIVES IN IT; AND THE MAIN POINT REQUIRED IN THIS LAW

TIMOTHY: Before God began to give His commandments, He first employed a preface which appears to apply solely to the people of Israel, as though He addressed His Law to none but them alone. However, it addresses us no less than this people, as we already concluded when we previously spoke of this matter in another place. Therefore I would like to better understand its meaning and the causes and reasons why God gave it this way and how it applies to us.

DANIEL: You know very well that when kings and rulers give some law and publish edicts and commandments in their name they are accustomed to affix some preface containing their name and titles by which they declare their majesty, lordship, and power. Wasn't it therefore suitable that when God, the sovereign King and Ruler of every creature and the "King eternal, immortal, invisible, the only wise God," to whom "be honour and glory for ever and ever," wished to reveal His Law, He declared Himself thus as Lawmaker and proclaimed His majesty? (1 Tim. 1:17.) Therefore He says: "I am the Lord thy God, which have brought thee out of the land of Egypt, out of the house of bondage."

For within this Law it is necessary above all to understand who the true God is and how He can be known, discerned, and distinguished from false gods. And this knowledge must precede all the following commandments (Ex. 20:2; Deut. 5:6). For who will call upon, fear, love, and place their trust in God if they do not first know Him? (Rom. 10:14.)

And this knowledge must not be the same as that of the pagans who, though they have some idea of some God whom it is fitting for them to call upon, fear, love, and honor, yet they do not know who He is or where to seek for Him (Gen. 21:22-34). And, because we cannot see Him or perceive Him with our eyes or other physical senses, therefore it is fitting for us to see, embrace, and speak with Him with heart and spirit and to consider and behold His Word as a mirror where He is clearly revealed to us, just as though we saw Him face to face and knew Him "even as (we are) also known," and no longer as through a glass darkly (1 Cor. 13:12).

THE NAME 'LORD' ATTRIBUTED TO GOD, WHICH IS 'JEHOVAH' IN HEBREW

TIMOTHY: Why does He first of all call Himself "the LORD?"

DANIEL: By the word which we translate *LORD* or *Jehovah* He declares in the Hebrew language (in which Moses wrote) His essence and nature, and that He is the Creator of all creatures, the "Alpha and the Omega, the beginning and the ending" (Rev. 1:8), which can be none other than Himself, through whom all things have their being, proceed from Him, and return to Him (Gen. 1:1; Isa. 44:24; John 1:1-3; Acts 14:15; 17:24). It is by Him that we live, move, and have our being. Thus He can rightly say "I AM," which no one else can truly say (Ex. 3:14; Isa. 47:8).

Therefore, because He is our Creator and therefore our Guide and Governor from whom we have received a soul, body, and goods, haven't we good reason to acknowledge Him as our King, Ruler, and Lord and render Him homage with our soul, body, goods and all we have received from Him, in perfect obedience? (Gen. 1:1; Ex. 13:8-9; Deut. 6:7; Matt. 22:44; 1 Cor. 4:4-5.) Therefore the Holy Scripture often reminds us of these things and ascribes to God the title of *Creator of heaven and earth* (Gen. 2:1-4).

From this we must conclude that no one except Him to whom this title and name apply can be our God, the eternal all-powerful Being, the Beginning, Sustainer, and End of all things. Thus by this name and title all false gods are excluded, for they cannot be gods because they are neither eternal nor self-sustaining.

And, seeing that we are the handiwork of this eternal God, we must not simply consider that He created us as the other visible creatures, but also that He created man truly in His own image and likeness, and all this world for us (Gen. 1:26-27). From this we must consider how many ways we are obligated to Him—indeed, when we have also received so many other blessings from Him as well.

IN WHAT SENSE GOD IS GENERALLY CALLED THE GOD OF ALL AND SPECIFICALLY THE GOD OF HIS CHOSEN PEOPLE

TIMOTHY: Why did He also say "*thy* God?"

DANIEL: It is because this first blessing is common to all men and to all creatures according to their nature because He created all (Rev. 10:6). Therefore He also adds this title to address Himself more personally to us. By this He provides us with His most intimate instruction which induces us to willingly receive it as from our Father who seeks nothing but our wellbeing and salvation by it (Jon. 1:16; Eze. 18:4; 1 Tim. 2:1-5). Therefore He not only says "God," but "*thy* God," which is a manner of speaking which, according to the style of the Holy Scriptures, carries with it His favor and grace.

For, firstly, the name of God which Moses here employs [Elohim] means in Hebrew *power* and *powers,* in order to declare to us that He has the power to aid us and that He is not only God for Himself—that is, who wishes to retain all good within Himself without communicating and distributing it—but that

His own role is to communicate these goods to men and to show Himself gracious and favorable toward them. When He does the contrary, being incited by man's wickedness and perversity, this work is called by His prophets a "strange work" (Isa. 28:21).

Therefore when He calls Himself the God of some people, He declares by this that He is not only their God as Creator of all—by right of creation, as He is the God of all creatures in general—but that He is also their God by the right of redemption. Nor is He severe and harsh like a judge toward wrongdoers, but gentle, kind, favorable, and merciful, as a good father toward his children (Gen. 15:15; Psa. 103:8-13). Thus, when He said "thy God," it calls to mind all He has already spoken, that He had chosen this people as His own inheritance and as a special treasure above all people (Ex. 19:5; Deut. 4:1-5; 10:15, 21-22).

Therefore He says by Isaiah: "But now thus saith the Lord that created thee, O Jacob, and He that formed thee, O Israel, Fear not: for I have redeemed thee, I have called thee by thy name; thou art Mine. When thou passest through the waters, I will be with thee; and through the rivers, they shall not overflow thee: when thou walkest through the fire, thou shalt not be burned; neither shall the flame kindle upon thee. For I am the Lord thy God, the Holy One of Israel, thy Saviour" (Isa. 43:1-3).

TIMOTHY: This is a good illustration of what you just said, and a very clear example.

DANIEL: Doubtless so. For you see that after He is said to be the God, Creator, Maker of Israel, and the Lord, He immediately adds: "thy Savior, who redeemed thee." And therefore Habakkuk also says: "Art Thou not from everlasting, O Lord my God, mine Holy One? we shall not die" (Hab. 1:12).

WHY GOD EXPRESSLY MENTIONED ISRAEL'S DELIVERANCE FROM THE LAND OF EGYPT IN THE PREFACE TO HIS LAW

TIMOTHY: And why did He then add: "I have brought thee out of the land of Egypt"?

DANIEL: He added this in order that they might better understand what I have just now explained and in order to keep this great blessing in mind which was recently received from Him, by which He openly declared Himself to be their God, taking them for His own peculiar people in a manner distinct from the Egyptians and all other peoples (Lev. 26:1; Deut. 7:6-9). Therefore, because of this singular favor, Israel had good reason to believe that such a good God and Father would only wish to set forth teaching that would be greatly profitable to them (Matt. 19:17).

Because of the lovingkindness and friendship God showed them, and because of His double right of lordship over them—first that of creation, and second the new act of deliverance which was like a new conquest in which He delivered them anew from the subjection of a cruel tyrant to make them His well-beloved, the firstborn of all peoples—He revealed Himself as a loving God whom His people could readily receive and embrace.

He therefore specifically declares: "I have brought thee out, and no other, by My sole strength and power, and not by your own power or that of any creature" (*see* Ex. 4:21; 15:13; Deut. 9:4; Hos. 11:1). And, not content with mentioning the land of Egypt only, He adds "from the house of bondage" to call to mind the work to which they had been pressed, and to let them understand that they were chained as a slave in hard bondage, living in bitter and tyrannical subjection, without having the form of a people as was afterward given by the Law and rule bestowed upon them by the Lord (Ex. 1:11-14).

TIMOTHY: This is well worth noting.

TWO

True God and False Gods

HOW THE REMEMBRANCE OF THE EXODUS FROM EGYPT IS A MARK DISTINGUISHING THE TRUE GOD FROM FALSE GODS

DANIEL: Also, this commemoration of the people's exodus from their Egyptian captivity not only contains the blessings which this people at that time received from God when He led them out of Egypt by His power, but also includes all the other works He accomplished in their midst by which He demonstrated and revealed Himself not only to be the true God but also the Leader and Protector of this people. Therefore, seeing that He could be neither seen nor perceived in a physical sense, He desired to give these visible testimonies of Himself by which He could be plainly seen by spirit and faith and be distinguished from false gods—particularly in Jesus Christ our Lord, in whom He is most openly revealed.

Therefore we are assured that when we address ourselves to this God who led the people of Israel out of Egypt—the same also who is revealed in Jesus Christ—we do not address an idol or a false god but the true God who is so declared by His works. For what people is there that can say of the gods they worship what we can say with truth of our God, the true God of Israel and Father of our Lord Jesus Christ?

And because men are so ungrateful toward God—there is nothing easier or more common than to forget His grace and blessings, for which the Spirit of God often reproaches His people—He ordained for Israel the sacrament of the Passover lamb, and to us that of the Lord's Supper, that we might remember Him by it.

TIMOTHY: When God thus recounts His blessings to His people, it seems to me that He also clearly declares that their ingratitude and wickedness will be utterly inexcusable if they ever abandon their God and revolt against Him and do not fear and reverence Him as their God and Lord and love and honor Him as their kind and loving Father.

DANIEL: You speak quite well. And therefore He says by His prophet Isaiah: "I have nourished and brought up children, and they have rebelled against Me. The ox knoweth his owner, and the ass his master's crib: but Israel doth not know, My people doth not consider," and by Malachi: "A son honoureth his father, and a servant his master: if then I be a father, where is Mine honour? and if I be a master, where is My fear?" (Isa. 1:2-3; Mal. 1:6.)

Seeing it is so, it is with good reason that God reigns over us, and that when He reigns, what was spoken by Isaiah is accomplished—that is, that there is no other light than His, indeed that "the sun shall be darkened in his going forth, and the moon shall not cause her light to shine" (Isa. 13:10; 24:23; 31:9; 60:19). Just as there is only one sun which gives light to the world, the light before which all others—both moon and stars—are eclipsed, so must it be with the one true God who reigns over us: we must receive and follow no other light but His. For, as it is written, we did not make ourselves, but rather "it is He that hath made us" (Psa. 100:3; 95:6).

And also: "For if we live, we live to the Lord; and if we die, we die to the Lord. Therefore, whether we live or die, we are the Lord's. For to this end Christ died and rose and lived again, that He might be Lord of both the dead and the living. . . . ye are not your own. For ye are bought with a price" (Rom. 14:8-9; 1 Cor. 6:19-20).

OF THE MANY TITLES GIVEN TO GOD IN HOLY SCRIPTURE, BOTH BEFORE THE EXODUS FROM EGYPT AND AFTER, AND PARTICULARLY SINCE THE COMING OF JESUS CHRIST IN THE FLESH, AND WHY THIS IS SO

TIMOTHY: This portion which mentions the exodus from Egypt is the most difficult in the entire preface. Therefore I would like to clearly understand why God expressly used this title and why He didn't instead use something more generic to all peoples, considering that this Law was given for all.

DANIEL: God could easily have used the most magnificent and most dreadful titles, but He preferred instead to use the most gracious and less appalling ones which would set Him forth to us as gentle and gracious instead of harsh and severe, in order that He might not estrange us from Himself by terrifying us by the grandeur of His majesty (Mark 13:26). Instead He allured us to Himself by the gentleness of His mercy.

Secondly, He also took names and titles according to the times, places, and persons to whom He revealed Himself and according to the means and manners to which they were accustomed (Ex. 19:9-18; Deut. 32:4). And, because He greatly desired to reveal Himself more personally, He also took more specific titles in order that we might know Him more intimately and that we might not remain overcome by fear (as we would have been had we been left in such extensive contemplation of Him without having some limit to our spirit), in order to know Him in some more particular blessing and more worthy of His loving-kindness.

Before this exodus from Egypt He was often called "the God of Abraham, Isaac, and Jacob" because of the promise and the covenant made with them, whereas prior to that He was most commonly called "the God of heaven" and "Creator of heaven and earth" (Ex. 3:6, 15-16). After the exodus from Egypt He took this title until Christ's coming when, as it was spoken by the prophets, He would no longer be "the Lord who brought us out of Egypt," but "the Lord who brought us from all the earth and . . . blessed us with all spiritual blessing in the heavenly places in Christ, and has taken and delivered us from all evil" (Eph. 1:3-7). This was not done without good and just reason.

And then we must also consider what was then said, that is, that this commemoration of the deliverance from Egypt is used as a figure of the commemoration of all the blessings of God toward His people because it was the beginning by which He more excellently and clearly showed what care He took of His people and aided them in a more noticeable way than before. And since that time He has always pursued with His mercy all those who by Jesus Christ have been added and joined to this people. Thus Moses used the manner of speech most common to him, which was to indicate and include the whole by a part of it.

THE TRUE KNOWLEDGE AND REVELATION OF GOD AND HOW THE TITLES ASCRIBED TO HIM SERVE TO DRAW AND LEAD US TO HIM

TIMOTHY: Explain this to me a little more clearly.

DANIEL: You must understand that it is not enough for man to have some general concept, fancy, opinion, or consciousness of God in his understanding. But, on the contrary, he is required to know Him as He is revealed by His Word, particularly in Jesus Christ His Son. Otherwise he will be lost in the vanity of his own thoughts and will remain without God. For, since God cannot be known or understood in His divine essence or majesty (if we desire to have such knowledge as is needful for our salvation), it is necessary that we seek and meditate on Him where He has chosen to reveal Himself to us and by the means that He has given us. For, if we do otherwise, we forge for ourselves a vanity of our own imagination which is imagined or invented. And it will happen that, instead of discovering God, we will create strange gods which are not gods at all. Thus, seeking to serve God, we will instead serve the devil.

Therefore it is not enough for us to merely believe that there are gods, but that there is one only. And this is still not enough, but we must also believe that this God—who is the only true God—is the Creator of heaven and earth and of all things visible and invisible.

Furthermore, seeing that man is fallen in sin and that he is in need of restoration, it is also necessary to know that this same God who created us is also the One who desires to restore and save us, and by what means He has willed to do so.

We must recognize Him alone as our Creator, Conductor, Father, Savior, and Redeemer, and none other; and we must recognize in Him the blessing of our creation, which also includes His providence and our restoration and redemption. This is why He chose a specific people to whom He willed to reveal Himself in human flesh in His Son Jesus Christ, that by Him He might reveal His knowledge to all. Therefore whoever knows "the God of Abraham, Isaac, and Jacob" and "the God who brought the people of Israel out of the land of Egypt" knows the "God and Father of our Lord Jesus Christ," and is a true Israelite and a true son of Abraham, the father of all who believe, engrafted into and joined with the true people of God (Rom. 4:3, 16-24; Gal. 3:7; Eph. 1:3).

HOW ISRAEL'S DELIVERANCE FROM THE LAND OF EGYPT WAS A SHADOW AND FIGURE OF THE DELIVERANCE MADE BY JESUS CHRIST; AND HOW THE CHRISTIAN PEOPLE ARE INCLUDED BOTH IN THE PEOPLE OF ISRAEL AND IN THEIR DELIVERANCE

TIMOTHY: The Christian people then are the same people as the people of Israel.

DANIEL: Certainly. For, seeing that Israel was elected by God to act as a caretaker and treasurer of His Word and promises in order that they would be preserved for us and be completed in us, and were the shadow and symbol of the true things brought to us by Jesus Christ, there is no doubt that we will be included in them. And, seeing that this deliverance from the tyranny of Egypt was a figure of this other and greater deliverance which we have by Jesus Christ our Lord, no mention can be made of the former without calling to mind the latter.

And this gives us reason to consider that, if the people of Israel had great reason to embrace the Law given them by God and to apply it and obey Him through it, then for the one reason that they had to do this, we have a thousand, seeing that God revealed Himself by this deliverance made for us by His Son Jesus Christ our God even more favorably and incomparably more than was ever displayed to the Israelites. For, though they and we all possess the same Jesus Christ and the same means of salvation by Him, yet this salvation was much more clearly and more excellently revealed to us than to them, without shadows and symbols, and much more openly revealed in a greater power of the Spirit of God. Therefore, seeing that the spiritual Israelites and true Christians are only one people, we must understand that what is addressed and applied to one is also addressed and applies to the other (Eph. 5; Col. 3:10-11). This includes everything pertaining to the true spiritual obedience to God which God requires, which applies equally to both of them.

TIMOTHY: This Law is then an eternal and unchanging rule for us, in order that we might know the difference between good and evil, between what must be done and what not, in all things.

DANIEL: And therefore it is firstly in the Hebrew language called by Moses *Torah*, which includes both doctrine and teaching, in order that we might understand that the Lord instructs and teaches us by this Law in all good things and that it is a sufficient, complete, and perfect instruction before which we must stop and rest ourselves, without seeking any other more complete or more perfect instruction.

THREE

The Difference Between Divine and Human Laws

THE TESTIMONY GOD GIVES US WITHIN HIS LAW, BOTH OF HIMSELF AND HIS NATURE; AND THAT OF MAN AND HIS REDEMPTION

DANIEL: Besides all this, you must also note that God here gives us a certain testimony that He is a true God and that He is wise, good, just, true, complete, and perfect. For it is clearly evident that the order proposed in this Law and the difference it places between good and evil and virtue and vice are not given haphazardly, but proceed from a determined counsel and a deliberate providence of God.

Furthermore, He also testifies that He is a just Judge who neither terrifies the righteous nor leaves the wicked unpunished, and who will not tolerate iniquity.

Also, in showing by His Law who He is, He also shows what human nature ought to be, and for what end it was created, and how it has fallen from the perfection in which it was created and is estranged from the will of God to which it must be conformed in order to reach and attain the end for which it was created.

Moreover, it also clearly teaches by this same means the salvation which He prepared for us in Jesus Christ through the Gospel. For, just as He did not create men to damn them one and all, so He also did not give this Law in vain merely to condemn men (which it would truly do if He had not ordained another means for their salvation).

HOW THE LAW OF GOD INCLUDES MORE IN SUBSTANCE THAN THE WORDS APPEAR TO SIGNIFY AT FIRST GLANCE; AND HOW IT MUST BE UNDERSTOOD ACCORDING TO THE NATURE OF THE LAWGIVER

TIMOTHY: The words contained in this Law must then include and mean much more than at first glance appears.

DANIEL: They contain all that I say.

TIMOTHY: Then there are many who neither know nor properly understand what they think they know and understand.

DANIEL: Indeed, I think there are none at all who differ from what you say. For whoever knows and properly understands this Law also knows and understands the entirety of the writings of the prophets and apostles. Thus we must not measure the matter mentioned in this Law according to the brevity of the words by which it is set forth but according to the substance contained within it and the nature and majesty with which it speaks and sets a thing forth. For, seeing that it is God who speaks, we can truly understand that His speech is couched in a lofty knowledge and wisdom and that there is neither a word nor syllable which does not bear great weight, power, and much meaning (Rom. 1:1-4; 2 Cor. 3:1-8; Eph. 4:4-5).

Also, seeing that "God is a Spirit" and a spiritual and eternal Essence without beginning or end, who desires to be worshiped "in spirit and truth" with a worship suitable to His nature and majesty, we can truly understand that there is a great difference between the nature of His Law—which is divine—and that of human laws, and that He is not content by its observance in the same manner that men content themselves with the observance of their laws (John 4:23-24).

THE DIFFERENCE BETWEEN DIVINE LAW AND HUMAN LAWS AND THE THINGS REQUIRED IN THEM; AND THE JUDGMENT OF GOD AND OF MEN REGARDING THIS MATTER

TIMOTHY: Tell me then the difference between them.

DANIEL: Men are content if their commandments are kept by external obedience and if nothing done against them comes to light. They do not concern themselves with passing judgment on the hearts, desires, and thoughts because they cannot be known unless they are revealed externally. However, even though they externally reveal themselves, yet they do not always condemn or punish them, or many other external works, even though they are very evil.

TIMOTHY: Why is this?

DANIEL: It is because men generally content themselves with maintaining human society in an earthly peace and tranquility because they often do not consider what is evil to be evil. Or, if they do consider it evil, they do not consider it to be as heinous as it is. Or, if they think it heinous, they tolerate it.

TIMOTHY: And from what does this fault proceed?

DANIEL: It proceeds in part from the ignorance and blindness of man's understanding caused by sin, which is the reason why he cannot discern between good and evil or judge one from the other as well as he could if he had remained in the state of innocence and grace in which he was created.

There is also another great evil: man willingly tolerates in others what he wishes to have tolerated in himself, and he is never so concerned with what touches the honor of God as he is with what concerns himself. This is the reason why men often punish more severely the crimes which concern their own honor or dishonor or their own profit or loss rather than those which directly battle against God's honor and majesty.

But it is not the same with God, for He is not content with mere external actions, but also requires an obedient heart, and looks to the source from which the work proceeds. He cannot be pleased with a work, no matter how lovely an appearance it might have, unless it proceeds from the heart and unless the heart is pleasing to Him. Again, the heart can in no way please

Him except when it approaches His nature and is conformed to His image and regenerated by His Holy Spirit. For no work is good or pleasing to God unless it proceeds from Him and is worked by Him. For "there is none good but One," and "every good gift and every perfect gift is from above" (Matt. 19:17; Jam. 1:17). Therefore the work which proceeds from us cannot please Him unless it is worked in us by His Holy Spirit and unless our spirit is led by His. For He who is a Spirit is only served in spirit (John 4:23).

HOW THE WORDS OF GOD'S LAW MUST BE UNDERSTOOD; AND HOW GOD LOOKS NOT ONLY TO EXTERNAL WORKS, BUT TO THEIR SOURCE; AND WHAT GOD APPROVES OR CONDEMNS IN MAN

TIMOTHY: From what I understand by your words, this Law is well worthy of being studied more closely than we imagine.

DANIEL: Yes, indeed. For, when God requires something of us that appears to apply to an external work, we must understand the whole by the part, the cause by the effect, the root and the tree itself by the fruit, the worker by his work, and all circumstances and connections the one by the other. And when He forbids one thing, we must also understand that He commands its opposite, and likewise that by commanding He forbids the contrary of what He commands. For He sees the whole man, his length and breadth, and probes his heart and all his thoughts and desires, and only approves in him what He finds of Himself and what He Himself has commanded, and condemns only what man has taken from anything other than Himself and what He has forbidden (1 Chr. 28:8; Psa. 7:11-13, 16; Acts 1:6-7, 15-20).

Therefore He not only condemns the work which appears evil outwardly, but also the source from which it proceeds. And He not only condemns when the fruit is brought to light, but even when it is hidden and concealed in the dark and gloomy abyss of the human heart, inscrutable to man but known and uncovered before God (Jer. 11:20; 17:9-10). Therefore David said: "O Lord, Thou hast searched me, and known me. Thou knowest my downsitting and mine uprising, Thou understandest my thought afar off" (Psa. 139:1-2). For how can man be hidden from the Worker who made him and knew him before he was begotten and made? Doesn't the Worker know His own work?

TIMOTHY: Who can know it, if He does not?

A CONSIDERATION OF THE THINGS WHICH ARE RIGHTLY DISPLEASING TO GOD IN MAN, AND FIRSTLY IN HIS WORK, AND THE WAY OF CONSIDERING IT AS COMMANDED OR FORBIDDEN BY GOD

DANIEL: Therefore, seeing that God is the Worker and has Himself fashioned and supplied the matter from which man was formed and has Himself given him his form, doubtless He knows very well who he is, what is within him, and what has been done by others to deface His work. And therefore John says: "the Son of God was manifested, that He might destroy the works of the devil," which is the sin which is in man by the wickedness of the devil (1 John 3:8).

Thus we must here note that there are four things within us which cannot please God and which each alone merit eternal death and damnation. For, if each one taken singly (if one could be separated from the other) is so abominable by nature and worthy of such grievous punishment, how much more must it be when all are joined together?

TIMOTHY: They must be very wicked indeed. But what are these things?

DANIEL: First is evil desire; second, the affections and passions begotten by it; third, the willful consent to this affection; and fourth, the execution of it in deed.

But I will begin my explanation with the last—that is, the deed which appears outwardly—so that by this we might have a better understanding of the preceding things which are more hidden and secret. In this point I will begin with the most obvious fruit by which we can easily judge the nature of every tree. For, in putting the deed first, not only can the worker be known by it, but also the forge and factory in which the work was done.

As for the deed, we must first consider it in two ways: the one as commanded by God, the other as forbidden. What is commanded by God can never be evil (if it is taken in the sense and manner in which He commanded it and is applied to the end to which it pertains). On the other hand, what is forbidden, being considered in this same way, can never be good in any manner whatever.

BY WHAT STANDARD THE WORKS OF MEN MUST BE EXAMINED; AND THE DANGER OF FOLLOWING HUMAN REASON AND JUDGMENT

TIMOTHY: We must be very careful not to base our judgment on human reason and the opinions of men in such a matter.

DANIEL: Very true. For it often happens that men judge good what is evil and that they condemn what is approved by God and approve what is condemned by Him for the causes and reasons already set forth. For the sentence of God's judgment will not be given according to human counsel, reason, and opinions, but according to the pronouncement which God already made by His Word and Law, which will be the weight, balance, and standard upon which all human thoughts, words, and works will be weighed and ruled.

FOUR

Man's Works and the Law of God

TIMOTHY: From what you say, it follows that whoever does what is forbidden by God or fails to do what He commands deserves condemnation. Likewise, whoever keeps himself from what He has forbidden and does what He has commanded will receive praise as a good and faithful servant.

DANIEL: These two points of yours are worthy of note. For there are some who think they have truly satisfied God's Law if they turn from the things forbidden in it (indeed, even if it was only done in an external manner), without setting their hand to perform what is commanded.

On the other hand, there are others who think themselves at perfect liberty to dispense with listening to what is forbidden in the Law when they have done some part of what is commanded them, and who think that this serves as a recompense for the rest. But we must indeed walk in another uprightness and perfection with God, and apply here what Jesus Christ said: "These ought ye to have done, and not to leave the other undone" (Matt. 23:23). For it must apply as well here as anywhere. What is commanded must be done, and what is forbidden must also be avoided.

Therefore you are no less guilty before God's judgment by abandoning what is commanded than you are in doing what has been forbidden. For He who commands and He who forbids is always the same Lord, who will no more permit His majesty to be violated by one side than by the other.

Therefore, in doing something which has been commanded, do not think that this little good you have performed on the one side has compensated for the great evil which you have done on the other side. For, if you do some good, you have merely done your duty and have only done what was commanded you (Luke 17:10). But you have left even more undone; for how will the evil that you committed in doing what was forbidden be atoned for by this little good which you have done when the good itself is not sufficient to atone for the offenses committed by you in abandoning your duty?

TIMOTHY: I see this well.

WHY IT IS NOT ENOUGH TO SIMPLY MAKE AN APPEARANCE OF DOING THE WORKS COMMANDED BY GOD IF THEY ARE NOT DONE WITH THE INTENTION AND FOR THE SAME PURPOSE FOR WHICH THEY ARE COMMANDED; AND HOW HYPOCRISY DISPLEASES GOD

DANIEL: Secondly, in doing the actual deed commanded by God, you must be careful to note why you do it and in what manner of heart. For if you do it more for your own glory and gain and love of yourself than for the honor of God and for the love which you bear Him or for your neighbor out of love for him, you make a good work an evil one and greatly offend Him by your hypocrisy, abusing His name by making a façade of His Law in order that you might serve yourself and your sinful desires through it. And by this such a deed is no longer a work of the Spirit of God because it is not done in truth but in falsehood. For all hypocrisy is deceit, seeing that it is nothing more than duplicity, guile, and deception, having one outward appearance while the truth of the matter remains within. All such deceptions proceed from the devil (John 8:44).

Thus, work done with deception is from the devil, not God. Therefore it can be no more pleasing to God than when the devil speaks the truth to cover his lies and when he transforms himself into an angel of light, and all the works he does, no matter how lovely an appearance they may have, although God turns them to His glory. For the intention is always evil, in that he never does anything except for himself, with regard neither for the honor of God nor for the good of any creature at all.

Therefore evil is never worse or more dangerous than when it has an appearance of doing good, for by this God is most dishonored and the most injury is done to men, seeing that it is most covered and veiled and most difficult to recognize and be discovered. Therefore those who call a hypocrite a "white devil," a devil masked and transfigured, have good reason to speak the way they do.

This is why false prophets are never more dangerous than when they have the greatest appearance of holiness and when they most believably counterfeit the true servants of God. It is the same with all hypocrites. Thus the good work that they seem to do is often more damaging than if they clearly revealed their true identity. This is why Jesus Christ condemned the almsgivings, prayers, and fasts of the scribes and Pharisees, and all their other works, because they only did them to be seen by men (Matt. 6:1; Luke 11:42-52).

WHETHER THE HEART OF MAN CAN SATISFY THE LAW OF GOD OR NOT; AND WHETHER IT CAN BE CONDEMNED OR ABSOLVED BY IT WITHOUT THE WORKS WHICH GOD REQUIRES OF MAN IN IT

TIMOTHY: Thus, if even a work which appears to be good cannot please God unless the heart from which it proceeds pleases Him, and seeing that the heart makes the work either pleasing or displeasing, I have three questions for you:

First, can God be satisfied with a heart without a work?

Second, can a man's work which in itself is evil please Him or be endured by Him when what is done does not proceed from an evil heart, but is done by constraint and against his heart, or done because he does not realize that it is evil?

Third, does God truly condemn an evil will that does not put its will into effect? And does this will displease Him as much as if the action were joined to it?

DANIEL: Concerning the first, it is certain that if God possesses a man's heart, He possesses his all. Therefore it is impossible for the heart to fail to offer and present to Him the work which He requires of it. We cannot separate the work from the heart any more than we can separate the fruit from the tree. For, just as every good tree cannot fail to bear its fruit in its time and season, so also the good heart will bear fruit in every time and season which God requires of it (Psa. 1:3; Matt. 12:33). If it doesn't, the reason is this: either it possesses neither the means nor the power to do so, or it lacks the desire. If it has the desire but doesn't possess the power or the means and yet does have a good will, then God forgives it and accepts the good will for the deed.

It is also the same if the will is evil and has no power to put its evil will into execution. For not only is the evil work displeasing to God, but also the evil will and desire, so much so that if it proceeds as far as it can and yet is unable to execute its evil desire, and nothing prevents it but a lack of power, there is no doubt that God sees the iniquity as already accomplished. Therefore our Lord Jesus Christ (and John, following His teaching) equates murder with him who hates his brother, and considers as an adulterer whoever who looks at his neighbor's wife with an evil and adulterous desire (Matt. 5:28; 1 John 3:15). We must understand the same of all other evils according to the interpretation of God's Law given to us by our Lord Jesus Christ Himself and His apostles after Him.

But, if a heart possessed the means and the power to do what is commanded and not only does not wish to but even more does not use every means to find an opportunity to do it, this is a certain witness that it is not good and that it lacks a good will. For, if it were good and if the will were such as it should be, it would hold nothing more precious than to render to God the obedience, honor, and service which is its duty and which God requires of it. Therefore God cannot be satisfied with such a heart, for it is unworthy and unbelieving.

IT IS IN VAIN FOR MEN TO BOAST IN THEIR GOOD HEART AND FAITH IF THEY DO NOT RENDER ANY TESTIMONY OF THEM BY THEIR WORKS; AND WHY THE JUDGMENT OF GOD WILL FALL UPON THEM; AND WHY THE PROPHETS REQUIRE THESE THINGS WHEN EXHORTING THE PEOPLE OF GOD TO REPENT

TIMOTHY: Thus we boast of the goodness of our heart in vain if our work does not testify to it.

DANIEL: This is just the same as it is with faith. Therefore we can here say like James: "Show me your heart and your faith by your works. For as faith without works is not true faith, but only a vain, fake, and dead faith and a false appearance of faith possessing no more of the true faith than a name without its effects, so also a heart can neither live for God nor be devoted to Him if it does not declare as much by its good works" (*see* Jam. 2:14-20). For a fire, however small it may be, cannot exist without light and heat—or, at the least, without a little smoke.

Therefore the method of God's judgment (as set forth by our Lord Jesus Christ) always speaks of the works by which this judgment is meted out to each man, because it is this which bears testimony to every man's heart and faith (Matt. 25:31-46; Rom. 14:16-19; 1 Cor. 4:5). Similarly, when the prophets call the people to true repentance, they always place strong emphasis on works, particularly those which concern one's neighbor, because hypocrisy is less able to disguise itself in this; and in order that a man might show how his heart stands towards God and in what reverence he holds the commandments of the first Table by how he regards the commandments of the second Table and his neighbor.

For it is very easy to boast of having a right heart before God and to show the same by the observance of external ceremonies. But when it is a matter of setting the hand to the work, that is, to "love from a pure heart," which is "the end of the commandment" and its works, which are the chief things that God requires, then the hypocrisy of the heart reveals itself (1 Tim. 1:5). Therefore John said: "But whoso hath this world's good, and seeth his brother have need, and shutteth up his bowels of compassion from him, how dwelleth the love of God in him?" (1 John 3:17.)

And again: "If a man say, I love God, and hateth his brother, he is a liar: for he that loveth not his brother whom he hath seen, how can he love God whom he hath not seen? And this commandment have we from Him, that he who loveth God love his brother also" (1 John 4:20-21).

By these words John clearly shows that there is no better way to know what affection our heart has toward God than by what it displays toward our neighbor and brother (who is the son of God and bears His image just as we do), and that there is no better means of unveiling hypocrisy and deceit within the human heart. For we can judge the love we bear the father by how we treat the child.

Therefore the prophets gladly use these arguments to convince the hypocrites. And our Lord Jesus Christ, in this form of judgment we already discussed, declares that He regards all to have been done to His own person which was done to His own people, whether it was good or evil (Matt. 25:40, 45). And, by this manner of proceeding, what we have said is clearly revealed. For when He reproached the hypocrites and reprobates because He had been rejected and mistreated by them, they immediately responded by demanding when this was done, as if they did not know. By this they openly declare that they wish to enjoy the reputation of having borne great love to Jesus Christ and of having fulfilled their duties to Him. But He convinces them of the contrary by the testimony they bore to His poor members, in the person of whom He attests that He has been rejected and mistreated, just as He declares that he was persecuted by Saul in the persecution which he made against the Christians (Acts 9:5).

FIVE

Free Will and Sin

HOW THE BASENESS AND FALSENESS OF THE HUMAN HEART IS REVEALED BY THE TRANSGRESSION OF GOD'S LAW; AND HOW NEITHER IGNORANCE, CONSTRAINT, NOR SOME OTHER REASON CAN EXCUSE IT

TIMOTHY: I think that this is also one of the main reasons why God sets forth the deed rather than anything else in this Law, in order that we would not deceive ourselves by the deceitfulness of our heart.

DANIEL: It is clearly so. For, just as the heart cannot pride itself with being good if it does not confess with the mouth and display by deed the faith and love of which it seeks to boast itself, so also it cannot excuse itself by declaring that it is not evil and therefore displeasing to God when it practices the evil forbidden by God. For it commits it either out of ignorance or presumption. If it acts out of ignorance, it is a witness that the heart is by nature evil. For, if it were not evil, it would not bear such fruit in any manner at all and would not be thus ignorant of the will of God. For such ignorance is a testimony to the darkness which sin engenders in the understanding of man, in contempt of God, and of the negligence in man to inquire into His will, as we have already more fully discussed in another place.

If, however, man sins knowingly and deliberately, what can he give as an excuse? Can he say that it was done against his will and that he did it by constraint? But by what constraint? If this reason were sufficient to excuse man's sin, there would be no sin that would not appear worthy of excuse, for it appears that there is no sin committed which has not been committed by constraint because of the fact that man is so corrupted by sin and so subjugated by the devil that by nature he can do nothing but sin. Therefore Paul says: "For the good that I would I do not; but the evil which I would not, that I do. . . . I am carnal, sold under sin," indeed, a slave of sin; "I see another law in my members" repugnant to the Law of God (Rom. 7:19, 14, 23). For, as our Lord Jesus Christ also said: "Whosoever committeth sin is the slave of sin" (John 8:34).

HOW SIN IS TRULY VOLUNTARY; AND THE DIFFERENCE WHICH MUST BE MADE BETWEEN "CONSTRAINT" AND "NECESSITY"

TIMOTHY: If this were the case, sin would not then be sin at all, for it would not be voluntary. And it is commonly said that all sin is voluntary, else it would not be deserving of punishment.

DANIEL: There are many things to consider on this point. The first is the difference which must be placed between *necessity* and *constraint.* For through lack of this distinction many are greatly deceived in the matter of free will and predestination and in the consideration of the nature of sin. For, properly speaking, we must say that we all sin by necessity, but not by constraint.

TIMOTHY: What difference is there between *necessity* and *constraint?* It seems to me that they are the same.

DANIEL: Yet there is a great difference between them. But, to properly understand this, we must first understand in what sense and in what way these words must be taken.

First, the word *necessity* is commonly taken as a lack of something we need, so that we often mean by it *indigence, poverty,* and *want.* But we do not properly use it in this way when we speak of the necessity by which man is induced to sin by his natural corruption, except that we can say that he sins by necessity—that is, by a lack and want of goodness, justice, innocence, holiness, and other virtues, gifts, and graces of God, of which he has been despoiled by the sin to which he is subject.

TIMOTHY: How then do you understand this word in this matter?

DANIEL: I understand it as a necessary consequence which follows from causes joined with their effects which, because of the nature of the causes and the things thus joined with them and dependant upon each other, they cannot be separated.

TIMOTHY: Give me an example of what you say.

DANIEL: Take the sun: its very nature is to shine and to give us day by its light. I say therefore: "The sun shines; it must be day." That is, it must be day, and nothing else. For its nature is such and it necessarily produces such an effect of its own nature without constraint or any violence. Therefore it naturally possesses the cause in itself.

But, where constraint exists, there is some act of violence which comes from outside of the thing forced and constrained, as when a woman is violated by force and must not be considered a harlot in the same way that we think of those who consent willingly to debauchery.

We thus sin both necessarily and by necessity, for it is impossible for us to do otherwise by nature, considering the corruption within us—unless we are regenerated by the Spirit of God—because of the natural corruption that sin has engendered in the whole human race.

However, nothing constrains us to sin except our own wicked and evil will which, being evil, cannot give itself to anything but evil. Therefore Job had good reason to say: "Who can bring a clean thing out of an unclean? not one" (Job 14:4). For this reason he previously said: "If I wash myself with snow water, and make my hands never so clean, yet shalt Thou plunge me in the ditch, and mine own clothes shall abhor me" (Job 9:30-31).

Eliphaz also speaks similarly: "What is man, that he should be clean? and he which is born of a woman, that he should be righteous? Behold, He putteth no trust in His saints; yea, the heavens are not clean in His sight. How much more abominable and filthy is man, which drinketh iniquity like water?" (Job 15:14-16.) He here shows us that man is steeped in sin and delights in it just as a fish feeds on water.

It is with good reason that the Lord spoke by Hosea: "O Israel, thou hast destroyed thyself, but in Me is thy help" (Hos. 13:9). It thus follows that our evil will works evil by necessity, for it is evil by nature and cannot do otherwise, just as we say that "a corrupt tree bringeth forth evil fruit" because its nature is evil (Matt. 7:17). As it is written: "That which is born of the flesh is flesh, and that which is born of the Spirit is spirit" (John 3:6).

But at the same time the will would not be a will if it did not act voluntarily and not by constraint. For will and constraint are opposites. Therefore will ceases where constraint exists, and it is not possible for the will to be constrained, but it can truly be corrupted and changed from good to evil or from evil to good.

Therefore, just as the good will necessarily works good because it cannot do otherwise, it clearly displays that "every good tree by necessity brings forth good fruit." However, it does this not by constraint, but voluntarily. So also the evil will, because it is evil, by necessity works evil because its nature is such that it cannot do otherwise. However, it does not do so by constraint, but voluntarily. For no external force or violence constrains and forces it against its will, for it itself is the very source and cause of the wickedness proceeding from it.

EXAMPLES AND ILLUSTRATIONS TO DISPLAY THE DIFFERENCE BETWEEN "NECESSITY" AND "CONSTRAINT"

TIMOTHY: I still do not quite understand this difference.

DANIEL: I'll explain it a little more clearly by examples and illustrations.

Fire by necessity heats and illuminates. It cannot do otherwise because that is its nature, and yet it is not constrained to do this. Water, to the contrary, by nature refreshes and moistens, and cannot do otherwise for the same reason.

A living being breathes, moves, and feels, and cannot do

otherwise. To the contrary, a dead body is deprived of all these things and can by necessity produce nothing but decay; yet neither the one nor the other are done by constraint, unless we wish to call constraint the inherent nature of these things.

TIMOTHY: Because these illustrations and comparisons are nearly all taken from things without will, give me some others more suitable to our purpose.

DANIEL: I will do so also. We cannot doubt that God is by necessity good, just, wise, holy, all powerful, and perfect, for He cannot be otherwise, nor can He do anything but what is good, righteous, wise, and holy. However, He cannot be constrained in the least.

Likewise the angels, inasmuch as they are angels (those who have persevered in the nature in which they were created by God), by necessity cannot do any other thing than praise God and serve and glorify Him. For, if they did otherwise, they would no longer be angels in the state in which they were created by God, but to the contrary would be devils, just as their companions who were cast out of their original state. And if they did what they do by constraint, and not voluntarily, they would not have praise from God, and He could receive no more pleasure from them than He does from the good that the devil is constrained to do inasmuch as God, in spite of his evil will and evil works, turns all to serve for His glory.

To the contrary, the devil, being what he now is (cast from the angelic state in which he was created by God), can by nature do nothing but evil, and dishonor God. For if he did otherwise, he would no longer be the devil. Yet he does not work evil by constraint, but voluntarily. For who constrains him to do evil? Does God, who forbade and condemned him and who can work nothing but good? It is clearly seen that he has no other constraint than his own evil will which takes pleasure in working evil just as the heavenly angels take pleasure in working good. But this is not the same as the good which the devil works, for he works nothing by constraint, nor does he commit any evil except that which proceeds from himself. Nor can he do any good except what God by His power and infinite goodness in spite of him turns to good, and by making his evil serve another end than what the devil intended.

TIMOTHY: I now begin to understand this a little more clearly than I did before.

THE FREE NECESSITY TO DO GOOD WHICH EXISTED IN MAN BEFORE THE FALL; AND THE NECESSITY—NOT THE CONSTRAINT—HE NOW HAS TO DO EVIL, INTO WHICH HE HAS FALLEN BY THE FALL; AND IN WHAT SENSE THE WORD NECESSITY MUST BE TAKEN WHEN IT REFERS TO GOOD THINGS

DANIEL: We can easily see by these examples what judgment we can make of man regarding this point we are discussing at present. For, after man was created by God—inasmuch as God created him good, righteous, and holy—he by nature and voluntarily did all for which he was created by God. For, seeing that God created him good, as all His other creatures, his natural disposition was to do good. And, remaining in this state and being joined with God and hearing His voice, he could not do otherwise. For, when his will was good, he could neither desire nor do anything but good (following this good will).

But, by giving heed to the devil's counsel and by changing his will and nature by following him, man fell into another necessity wholly contrary to the first. For, instead of working good by nature and being wholly devoted to God as he was beforehand (for of his nature he could neither wish nor do otherwise), now, to the contrary, having changed in nature and will, he could follow nothing but his nature.

We see once again something similar to this in the darkness which night brings, and in what follows. For what is the cause of the night? Isn't it the darkness of the earth which removes the sun's light and brings us darkness, which is the opposite of this light, by means of which the day is turned to night? And we, being in the night, cannot do what we do in the day, nor walk in the right path, but rather the opposite. This is because we have darkness instead of light, without which we cannot find the right way.

Nevertheless, necessity is always without constraint. For, though the lack which exists in man (which we call *necessity)* can by chance give him an opportunity to induce him to steal, yet he cannot rightly say that he was constrained to steal. For, if he were a good man and not a thief, he would have endured all miseries and deprivations rather than steal. But, because he prefers to live at ease rather than do his duty with some discomfort according to the will of God, he prefers to steal rather than to obey God.

SIX

God's Wisdom, Glory, and Mercy on Display

THE NECESSITY IN WHICH MAN HAS PLACED HIMSELF BY HIS SIN

TIMOTHY: By what you say I understand well what the nature and will of man would have been if he had remained in the original state in which he was created by God. For, regarding his will, it would necessarily have been regulated by God's will (as is currently that of the angels who remained steadfast), such that man would sin no more than the angels. And thus he would not have lost the liberty of his will nor done anything by constraint. And by this it would have been a good necessity, which proceeded from the riches of the goodness and grace which God had endowed and made him a partaker of.

But, when he turned from this way, it happened to him just as it did to the angels when they turned from God. And he showed by this that he was so created by God, good and just, with a good and holy will, though he was not created in such a way that he was and must be immutable in his own nature and power.

Therefore, seeing that man, by the seduction and counsel of the devil—who was the first transgressor—turned from the will and obedience of God his Creator and covenanted with the original transgressor and apostate who by pride and ingratitude made himself an enemy of God, he participated in the perversity of the devil, with whom he covenanted. Therefore his good and holy nature and will were corrupted and perverted and made like those of the devil, whom he received not only as a comrade but also as his guide, leader, master, and lord.

Thus, when previously remaining united and joined with God and having God within him and being led by His Spirit he could work nothing but good, unforced and unconstrained, now, to the contrary, being separated from God and joined to the devil and led and governed by him, he can do nothing but evil, by the working of his own will, without constraint of any but himself, solely because his nature is such. Because of this he now takes as much pleasure in working evil as he did in working good in his original state of innocence.

Now this necessity is very different than the first. For, unlike the original which proceeded from the abundant riches of God's grace, this proceeds from man's depravity and sin. Therefore it is as miserable as the first was blessed. It seems to me that this is what you wish to conclude.

DANIEL: You might understand this even more easily by the comparison of a healthy man with a sick one. Consider a man sound in body and mind, being completely whole and not corrupted by any diseases, with no desire or appetite for any food or drink except what is good and profitable to his nature and health and in such quality and quantity as his nature and health require, because he is thus disposed.

Now consider again that this same man, being sick, would be wholly contrary to what he was when well, because he is quite otherwise disposed. What is completely opposite would be the most appetizing to him, and he would indeed find no greater pleasure in anything as much as in that which would be most contrary to him, most polluted, and most strictly forbidden. Yet could he complain that he had been forced to be this way either by the physician or others who had forbidden him, and that his will had been forced by someone other than himself, who willingly perished because he was so weak that he could not overcome his own desires and corrupt nature?

TIMOTHY: This is clear enough.

THE MARVELOUS COUNSEL OF GOD DISPLAYED IN THE FALL AND RESTORATION OF MAN; AND HOW IT IS DIFFERENT OR SIMILAR TO THAT WHICH WAS REVEALED IN THE FALL OF THE WICKED ANGELS AND THE PRESERVATION OF THE GOOD ANGELS

DANIEL: What you say is true. And no one can doubt that man would have become exactly like the devil (to whom he united himself) if God had utterly abandoned and left him in the state to which he fell by his rebellion and ingratitude, just as He abandoned and left the devil. But God instead here employed a marvelous counsel and means. He did not allow the entire angelic nature He created to be destroyed, but rather preserved a part in such a way that they never participated in the transgression and corruption of the others. And, just as He preserved those who remained in their original state so that they cannot fall, so also He abandoned the others who fell so that they can never be restored, and never shall be (2 Pet. 2:4; Matt. 25:31).

But, to the contrary, He permitted the entire human race to fall and corrupt themselves and all human nature in the first man that He created—that is, in its very source (Rom. 5:12-14; 1 Cor. 15:21).

But, on the other hand, He displayed such moderation that He did not will that all those who were included in this fall be eternally lost as he who was the original cause of this fall—that is, the devil, who pulled down the first man into such ruin with himself. But, instead, the very moment the fall was committed by the devil's inciting, God instantly provided a remedy against this great evil and provided the means to restore His work and His creation which His adversary had ravaged.

This remedy He had prepared beforehand by the eternal counsel and settled purpose of His election, by which He elected and prepared in His Son Jesus Christ "the vessels of mercy" (Rom. 9:23), not only before this blow was struck in the body and person of the entire human race, but also before the creation of the world (Rom. 8:27-29; Eph. 1:3). By this He reveals both the justice of His judgment and His grace and mercy, and how He is the Author of all good, as opposed to His adversary, who is the author of all evil.

For, if God had restored the angelic nature which had fallen just as He restored the human nature, we could truly assume that the angels who fell had righted themselves or that their fall was not as grave and wicked as it was nor the sin so odious and detestable before God. Likewise His justice, grace, and mercy would not have been so well displayed. For He had good reason to allow the angel transgressors to bear everlasting witness against themselves of their transgression and rebellion, that He might make known in them how good it was to remain united to God and how evil to be separated from Him.

Man can judge by this what power and virtue he can have in himself to restore himself and save himself, considering the weight of God's wrath that the demons bear. For if these creatures who were created so excellent cannot bear such a burden or release themselves from it, though they are sunk even to hell, how can man, who is no more than a worm, and how can he deliver himself? And if "God spared not the angels that sinned, but cast them down to hell, . . . how shall we escape," unless it is by His grace and mercy alone? (Job 25:6; 2 Pet. 2:4; Heb. 2:3; 12:25.)

On the other hand, if He had permitted them both to fall and had left them all to the same damnation, His power, grace, and mercy would not be known as it now is. And if He had restored the ones and left the others, it might still appear that He lacked the power to preserve His creatures in the state in which He had created them, or that He was unable to care for them as He wished to. If He had done the same with man, it would seem to the contrary that He lacked the power or that He lacked the care and desire to restore the creature who had ruined itself, but only possessed the power to preserve and sustain him in his original state if he persevered in it.

But, by using the means He employed, He has shown all these things together:

First, there is no creature at all who can survive of itself, no matter how excellent it may be.

Second, He is well able in His power to preserve all in their state when it so pleases Him and to restore them even if they have fallen and sinned, though this cannot be done by any other means than by His power and grace alone.

Therefore, just as man can be restored and returned to his original state by His grace and mercy, so to the contrary, remaining in his natural state—as it is at present—he can by his wicked will do nothing but evil, though he has no other constraint than his own wickedness.

HOW ALL THAT WAS DONE BOTH IN THE FALL AND PRESERVATION OF THE ANGELS AND IN THE FALL AND RESTORATION OF MAN RETURNS TO THE GLORY OF GOD; AND HOW THIS REASON ALONE MUST CONTENT US IN THE MATTER OF PREDESTINATION

TIMOTHY: From what I can see, all that has been done in all these things always returns to the glory of God (to which must be added all the decrees of His providence), as the chief end to which He looks above all in all His works, and to which it is fitting that He rule all other ends.

DANIEL: You have understood and concluded well. This is why it is written that "the LORD hath made all things for Himself: yea, even the wicked for the day of evil" (Prov. 16:4), that is, that He might be glorified even in their evil. And Paul, speaking of the eternal election of God, says that He has "predestinated us unto the adoption of children by Jesus Christ to Himself, according to the good pleasure of His will, to the praise of the glory of His grace, wherein He hath made us accepted in the Beloved" (Eph. 1:5-6).

Seeing that it is so, what good reason can men find to take offense at the matter of predestination? Shouldn't the glory of God be preferred above all His creatures? And if all the creatures perish, why should we find this strange if God is glorified in their destruction and is thus pleased by it?

TIMOTHY: No one could find this strange unless they valued the creature more than the Creator.

DANIEL: Therefore we must not doubt that the offense that many take in the matter of the damnation of the reprobates proceeds indeed from no less than a great pride and arrogance of the flesh which takes upon itself more than it ought. For, if it prized itself as little as it is worth and if it prized God and His glory as much as it ought, not only would it not find it strange to understand that God has ordained to glorify Himself in the damnation of some, but when this same judgment must be passed even upon its own person, it would glorify God in His just judgment. It would never complain against Him for taking such proceedings and for testifying and pleading against it in order that it might uphold the cause of the reprobates, accusing Him as though He could do them wrong. But, what is even more, it would rather wish to be cast out itself, as Paul desired for the sake of his brethren the Israelites, if it were possible that this could be done and if God would be more glorified by it (Rom. 9:3).

From where then do our contrary thoughts proceed if not from the pride of our nature? For who are we? Where did we come from? What wrong has God done us? How can we accuse Him or ascribe to Him the guilt of our sins and damnation, making Him (instead of the devil) the author of sin? Considering the fact that He gave us some command, can we complain that some other force and violence constrains us to do evil besides our own wicked nature and desires? Perhaps we might wish to complain that He made us capable of sinning or that, having sinned, He did not show us all the same grace and did not save us all, seeing that He could truly do so if He desired—or else He would neither be God, nor all powerful. But He was pleased to do otherwise, and not without good and just reason, which never ceases to be such even though we cannot understand it.

Therefore we must always conclude with the prophets that our destruction is our own and our salvation is God's alone (Hos. 13:9), and say with Paul: "Nay but, O man, who art thou that repliest against God? Shall the thing formed say to him that formed it, Why hast thou made me thus? Hath not the potter power over the clay, of the same lump to make one vessel unto honour, and another unto dishonour? What if God, willing to shew His wrath, and to make His power known, endured with much longsuffering the vessels of wrath fitted to destruction: and that He might make known the riches of His glory on the vessels of mercy, which He had afore prepared unto glory?" (Rom. 9:20-23.) And again: "Oh, the depth of the riches both of the wisdom and knowledge of God! How unsearchable are His judgments, and His ways past finding out! For who hath known the mind of the Lord? Or who hath been His counselor? Or who hath first given to Him, and it shall be recompensed unto him again?" (Rom. 11:33-35.)

HOW THE WILL OF MAN CAN ONLY BE FORCED BY HIS OWN WICKEDNESS AND NOT BY ANYONE ELSE, NOT EVEN BY THE DEVIL HIMSELF

TIMOTHY: As for me, I agree with what you say, but yet you cannot deny that man is at least somewhat constrained to sin by the temptations and enticements of the devil.

DANIEL: This constraint you speak of is constraint without constraint, for it is not within the power of all the demons, or of all the creatures together, to force the will of a single man. Therefore whatever temptation and enticement man might happen upon, if he does not consent of his own will, he cannot be induced to do anything against that will. But it happens with him as with a harlot. If she is solicited by whoremongers and fornicators, she will give herself over to them, which a true woman would never do, but would resist all such solicitations and temptations and vanquish them. Therefore, though the harlot might ascribe a part of the guilt of the sin she has committed to those who entice and solicit her to do it, yet she cannot complain that she was constrained and thus excuse herself by this means. For, if she had not consented of her own will, she would not have been seduced. But, because her nature was already devoted to such things, these solicitations served as matches and oil, or as kindling thrown upon the fire, which can kindle or inflame no more than her nature is inclined and ready to participate.

Thus man is induced to sin by his own evil nature and desires which, being kindled and enticed by the devil, more clearly and openly reveals what his nature is (Jam. 1:13-15). Thus you can see how man always sins by his own will. And if he wishes to say that he was forced into doing a deed which he clearly knew to be against the will of God, he must consider in what force and violence it was done.

If he was so forced by the violence of another that he could not be master of his own members (though he resisted by all the means he could and declared by deeds and words that his heart and will in no way consented), he might be excused just as an honest woman who was taken by force who nevertheless cried out and resisted with all her power against her rapist, and who indeed would have been ready to lose her life rather than her chastity.

But if you work an evil work either to please men or out of fear of falling under their disfavor and indignation or of receiving some dishonor or earthly harm, you cannot in such a case allege any other constraint than your own evil will. You have no better excuse than Pilate, who condemned Jesus Christ because he was constrained by the fear of the Jews (Matt. 27:15-26; John 19:12-16).

For, if you love God with all your heart, and more than yourself, and if you prize His glory above your own and the soul more than the body and heaven more than earth, you would be quite content to lose what you fear to lose, and yet you would not lose anything at all, but to the contrary you will gain double. For, as Jesus Christ says: "Whosoever will save his life shall lose it: but whosoever will lose his life for My sake, the same shall save it" (Luke 9:24; Matt. 10:15-26; John 12:25). And by this you will not abandon God for the creature and will not exchange the inheritance laid up for you in heaven for an earthly inheritance, nor the blessing of God your Father for a mess of pottage, as did Esau, but on the contrary you would rather lose your life, which must not be valued as highly as the honor of God and the salvation of your soul (Gen. 25:29-34; Heb. 12:16).

SEVEN

Contradictions which Seem to Exist in God's Law

THE DIVISION OF ALL THE LAW INTO TWO TABLES, AND THE ORDER OF THE MATTERS SET FORTH AND CONTAINED IN THEM

TIMOTHY: I now know by what you say that all such excuses cannot excuse us before God. But why is it that God sometimes approves of works which He seems to have forbidden? He has commanded us to honor father and mother and to obey the magistrates, yet He sometimes highly praises those who do not obey them at all. He forbids murder, and then sometimes He praises the manslayers.

DANIEL: This difference comes from the nature of God's commandments and the order by which He has placed them in His Law. For He has gathered all and divided them into two Tables in which He has written and ordered His commandments according to the order and dignity of the matter each deals with.

TIMOTHY: Explain this order to me.

DANIEL: In the first Table He has written four commandments which chiefly and directly concern His glory, without any particular consideration for anyone but Himself (just like the first three petitions laid out in the Lord's Prayer). The second Table contains six commandments which concern the things which pertain to our neighbor. These must be governed by the first four, upon which they depend and to which end they must always look (just as the last three petitions of the Lord's Prayer must always be governed by the same end to which the first three tend). Therefore if in some case it happens that we must violate some commandment of the first Table to accomplish the second, the second Table must in such a case give place to the first, and we must have recourse to it to gain the true understanding and true purpose of what it contains.

THE MANNER OF HARMONIZING THE PASSAGES OF THE LAW IN THE HOLY SCRIPTURES WHICH APPEAR TO BE CONTRADICTORY TO THE COMMANDMENT GIVEN TO HONOR FATHER AND MOTHER AND THE LOVE AND HATRED WHICH MUST BE RENDERED THEM

TIMOTHY: How can this be? Has God given a Law which contradicts itself and which contains some commandments which cannot be observed without violating others?

DANIEL: No, if the Law is properly understood in the sense in which it was given by God. And, to better understand this difficulty, I will explain it to you by some easy examples. God commands me to honor my father. Why is this commanded me?

TIMOTHY: In order that God might be honored by the honor which we render our fathers by recognizing the blessings which we have received from Him by them, who are the instruments and ministers of His lovingkindness to us.

DANIEL: You have answered well. Thus you see how this commandment has its foundation in the first Table, so that by dishonoring your father you not only dishonor the man who is your natural father, but in dishonoring him you dishonor God your eternal Father, of whom your natural and earthly father is only an image and representative toward whom you display what affection you have for Him whom he represents. And, because this image deals with you more nearly and you are more closely related to it, and as much as God imparts more openly and more abundantly His lovingkindness by this instrument and makes His image shine more brilliantly in him, by so much is your ingratitude and iniquity more heinous.

But if it happened that your father were disloyal to God and that he required something of you which you could not obey without disobeying God, you are under no obligation, nor do you owe him anything in such a case, for you are exempted in such a case by the first Table and by its interpretation and true meaning. For, seeing that the honor you owe your father includes the honor of God and is founded on it, it is plain that if God is dishonored by what your father requires of you, you do not honor him at all (in the manner that it is commanded of God to honor him) by doing what is required by your father. For your father cannot be truly honored in what dishonors God, but to the contrary he is dishonored when God is dishonored (though men do not always know, understand, or recognize this).

Therefore, when your father makes some commandment, you must pay attention to the nature of the thing commanded by him. If you can obey him without violating your duty to God and your conscience, you must strive to please him as much as is possible for the honor of Him who has commanded you, no matter how great the difficulty of the thing.

But, if it be to the contrary, you must not acknowledge him in such a point as your father, for the devil requires by him that you render your father the honor that you owe to the only true God, and seeks to make you his instrument by your father. But flee this Satan transformed in the likeness of your father, and tell him that you have no father for whom you would abandon and renounce God your heavenly and eternal Father. For, if a father requires of his daughter that she deliver herself to him to make of her a harlot or to abuse her himself or to prostitute her to some whoremonger, must she recognize such a father as her father? And must she obey him in this?

TIMOTHY: No man possessing an ounce of good judgment would deny that the man who did this was worthy of the greatest punishment and that she who chose death rather than please her father in such wickedness would be worthy of greatest praise. For she would not be obeying her father in this, but instead a whoremonger, a lewd man, an execrable incestuous beast, and a true devil.

DANIEL: Well said. If then it is unlawful for a daughter to deliver up her body to her own father to abuse it by any vileness whatever, or to another even if it is by his command, how much less must it be lawful for the soul, which is much more precious than the body, to deliver itself to any creature at all in order to be joined with the devil?

If then your father wished to be an idolater and desired that you be one with him and that you abandon Jesus Christ to please him, you must then employ the interpretation that Jesus Christ made of this commandment concerning the honor which is due to a father and mother founded in the first Table, as we shall more amply show when we come to the fifth commandment.

TIMOTHY: What interpretation do you speak of here?

DANIEL: Of what He said: "If any man come to Me, and hate not his father and mother" out of love for Him, as another evangelist puts it: "He that loveth father or mother more than Me is not worthy of Me," and such a person "cannot be My disciple" (Luke 14:26; Matt. 10:37). This is a very clear interpretation which shows us that it is a great virtue and praise to spurn father and mother at certain times—that is, in such cases as we have considered. For such a scorn of them is not scorn properly speaking, but only in man's judgment, any more than the hatred with which Jesus Christ desires us to hate them out of love for Him, which is not hatred, but true love, founded on the love of God. For we must judge these things according to their effects more than according to the feelings of men, according to which we consider them, as in many other similar passages.

It is written in Proverbs, in which Solomon speaks in the person of Wisdom: "all they that hate me love death" (Prov. 8:36). There are none who do not hold death in horror. However, seeing that he who despises and hates Wisdom is seeking his own death and ruin, doesn't it appear that he loves it and desires it and that he could do no more if he did desire it? It is also written: "Whoso is partner with a thief hateth his own soul," and again: "He that spareth his rod hateth his son" (Prov. 29:24; 13:24). No one, however, does this out of a hatred he bears for his soul, his life, or his child, but rather out of love, if we look only at the outward affection of the person. Yet the Spirit of God speaks the truth, as the effect so declares. Thus, just as they hate the truth who love folly and what they ought not, so also he loves truly who hates as he ought to hate and what he ought to hate.

The same can be said of honor and dishonor, but we needn't treat this point any longer, seeing that its place will be better suited to the commandment of which we have just spoken. Therefore I have only said this as an example.[1]

AN EXAMPLE TO THIS SAME PURPOSE IN THE COMMANDMENT REGARDING THE OBEDIENCE DUE TO RULERS AND IN THE COMMANDMENT GIVEN AGAINST MURDER

TIMOTHY: We could also, in my opinion, say the same of rulers and lords.

DANIEL: Peter and John teach us by their example that we must regard it so. For did they despise the commandment that commanded them to render obedience to rulers and magistrates when they rejected the admonitions of the Jerusalem Council given contrary to the commands of God when they responded: "We ought to obey God rather than men"? (Acts 4:19; 5:29.)

TIMOTHY: To the contrary, they fulfilled this much better than if they had done otherwise, and by this they showed its true meaning.

DANIEL: This is also why Phinehas received great praise from God because he killed the fornicator and the harlot. He was not rebuked for committing murder because he did not act out of hatred or murderous passion but out of the duty and obedience he owed God, whose honor could not be preserved unless such

[1] See Pierre Viret, *Honor Thy Father and Mother: A Study on Submission and Authority* (Psalm 78 Ministries, 2017).

wickedness was punished and revenged with such zeal (Num. 25:7-13).

You can thus understand by these examples how the work which can have some appearance of being evil before men and of being contrary to the commandments of God is in no way wicked in the sight of God. Neither is it condemned in the judgment of those who take the Law in its true sense and who know that they must govern the second Table by the first, and not by what is pleasing and conformable to their own will.

EIGHT

Sin and Its Consequences

THE SINS HIDDEN WITHIN THE CONSCIENCE AND EVIL WILL OF MAN; AND HOW WICKED DESIRE IS A SIN WORTHY OF DAMNATION BEFORE GOD; AND HOW IT DISPLEASES HIM

TIMOTHY: It seems to me that you have amply and clearly explained this matter of works. Let us turn now to the rest.

DANIEL: If what we have said of works is properly understood, the rest will be easy, for we can judge the will and desires by the same means God uses to judge the work.

If then you are incited to evil by some evil desire and your will also consents and agrees in such a way that nothing remains but the actual execution of the act, then the iniquity is already accomplished before God. By what we have already said, you know what judgment God will make.

If, on the contrary, there is such resistance in you that your spirit and will do not desire to agree with this evil desire which solicits you, but to the contrary they flee from it as far as they can, it is certain that the iniquity is not as great. However, such an evil desire—even if it is met with some resistance—cannot be free from sin because of the corrupt and wicked source from which it proceeds. For this is a sure witness that there is great poison and corruption within where such fruit buds, even though it encounters hindrances which prevent the buds and fruit from ripening to maturity.

Now such a corruption can only be greatly displeasing to God, considering that it proceeds from His adversary and that it is contrary to His holiness and majesty, as we see in the example of infants—indeed, even in those who not only are too young to commit any evil crime, but also who do not possess the discernment between good and evil. We see how death has power over them and carries them from the world. This could never be if they did not possess sin within themselves. For, seeing that sin brings forth death and that it is a fruit of sin's curse, we can be quite certain that where sin does not reign, death also can have no power, as Paul concluded so well (Rom. 5:10-12).

HOW, BECAUSE OF THIS EVIL DESIRE, WE ARE JUSTLY WORTHY OF DEATH AND DAMNATION EVEN FROM OUR MOTHER'S WOMB

TIMOTHY: What then is this sin in infants which is so displeasing to God that not only does He render them subject to physical death but also to eternal death, and makes them children of wrath and cursed even before they have the exercise of their reason to be able to know and discern either good or evil?

DANIEL: It is the natural corruption of which David speaks, saying: "Behold, I was shapen in iniquity; and in sin did my mother conceive me" (Psa. 51:5). Or, if we desire to express the sense of David's words even more clearly, we could say (following the Hebrew meaning): "And my mother warmed herself of me in sin," or "with sin." By this we are shown that he was begotten, conceived, and nourished within his mother's womb in sin as if he and sin were twin brothers begotten, conceived, and nourished together in the womb of the same mother. Thus it is easy to understand how sin is now natural to man (being in this corrupt nature in which he fell by his transgression), for what David says of himself pertains to the entire human race. Thus the conception he speaks of in this passage is common to all.

Therefore, just as a young snake is abhorrent to us not only the instant it is born but even if it still lies in its egg or in its mother's womb, so also we are justly displeasing to God from the very womb of our mother. And why is it that we abhor this young snake? Isn't it because of the venomous nature within it? For, though its nature has not yet revealed itself, yet it lacks nothing and it shall not fail to reveal its nature (unless it lacks the means to do so), but it shall truly reveal itself in its time.

TIMOTHY: Is it the same with man?

DANIEL: We cannot doubt it, for experience shows it quite clearly. From the time our first father was empoisoned with the venom of the old serpent, he could only beget children like himself and give life to young snakes of the same nature as he was and infected with the same venom. This venom, though it remains hidden some time within us, shall not indeed fail to instantly reveal itself at the first occasion it can find. This is the first source, the first foundation, and the first cause (with regards to man) of all the sins that he can commit.

Now if this evil source—no matter how hidden and concealed it might be—is so displeasing to God that it already merits eternal damnation before it has even budded, how much more must He be displeased with its blossoms, branches, and the entire tree with its fruits?

TIMOTHY: It is easy to judge.

DANIEL: Nothing could be easier.

THE DEGREES OF SINS AND THEIR ROOT AND FRUITS; AND THEIR CONCEPTION AND CONSUMMATION

TIMOTHY: It seems that, by the conclusion you make, we could easily distinguish and discern between all the degrees of sin.

DANIEL: It is quite simple to do so. This first source and natural corruption with its inclination and nature always given to evil is what we commonly call *original sin,* which by nature is wholly damnable and irresistible to man unless he is delivered from it and regenerated by the grace of the Spirit of God alone.

Next, the evil desire which awakens in man and entices him to evil is like the bud of this corrupt root and accursed source, which is always shooting forth some such bud no matter how sanctified the man might be as long as he is in this world wrapped in this body of sin, his outward man, and his old Adam. Thus it follows that there is no man living—as holy as he may be—who is not still a great sinner before God—indeed, even if he had in himself no other offense than this (John 1:29; 1 John 2:1-2). Thus we always have good reason to say with all the Church: "Forgive us our sins" (Matt. 6:12; Luke 11:4).

If this bud proceeds as far as to a decision and to producing a consent of the will, the rebellion is always more greatly revealed and the sin grows to an even greater degree and is more complete than before. Now if the man, having come this far in his sin, recognizes his offense and before proceeding further turns and begs pardon of God, he is less guilty than he who continues as far as to put his evil will into effect or who continually persists in it even though he cannot accomplish it and is truly grieved that he cannot put it into execution. But he who feels open repugnance in his conscience against the evil which solicits him and yet scorns the warning God sends him by his own conscience and gives in to his evil desire is even more guilty than he who was surprised either by ignorance or by weakness.

THE OPINION OF THOSE WHO SAY THAT NONE WILL BE DAMNED, AND THE ABUSE OF GOD'S MERCY IN THIS, AND THE MAGNITUDE OF SIN

TIMOTHY: What you say is quite contrary to the opinion of those who say that none will be damned and that even the devils themselves will one day be saved.

DANIEL: If this is so, then the word of God—which speaks to the contrary—will thus be found to be a liar.

TIMOTHY: They place their foundation on the mercy of God, saying that God created no one to lose them and that it would be a great cruelty of Him and quite contrary to His merciful nature to punish a temporal sin so rigorously—that is, with everlasting punishment.

DANIEL: Such persons greatly deceive themselves and openly show that they know neither the nature of sin nor the majesty of Him against whom it is committed. Do they count as nothing the contempt of such majesty, according to which the greatness of their sin must be measured and not only according to the thing in which it was committed? And if it is a question of the manner in which God is offended by sin, it is indeed the greatest that it can be. For can man commit any theft, sacrilege, robbery, treason, cowardice, or wickedness greater or more heinous than to revolt against God and his Creator and to endeavor to rob Him of His divinity and place himself in His stead?

TIMOTHY: Was there ever a man in the world who could have been so presumptuous to even think—I dare not say attempt—what you say?

DANIEL: To give you some examples, we must simply begin with the first man and then proceed as a result to all the others.

TIMOTHY: Do you mean to say that Adam committed such a sin when he ate of the fruit of the tree which was forbidden him?

DANIEL: Why then do you think that God was so enraged against him and condemned him to such grievous punishment? Do you suppose it was merely because he stole some apple or pear as children steal from a garden, and ate it with his wife?

TIMOTHY: I think indeed that the offense is very grievous when it is nothing more than disobedience and the contempt of the majesty of God, just as you mentioned. But what more must be considered in this?

DANIEL: We must also consider the horrible sacrilege committed against the divinity of God which I just mentioned. For the devil convinced Eve (by which Adam then afterwards was induced to follow his counsel) that, far from perishing in death as God had warned them if they ate of the fruit of the tree which had been forbidden them, to the contrary they would be made like God. And he stated that, because God feared this and because of the envy He bore them (in order that they might not share in such a great good), He gave them this commandment (Gen. 3:1-22).

And, therefore, when God rebuked Adam for his transgression and exposed his offense, He spoke in mockery in order to more greatly humble him and to more clearly show him his foolhardy action and the confusion and misery into which he sank himself with all his race, having preferred to follow the counsel of the devil rather than the commandment of God his Creator: "Behold, the man is become as one of Us" (Gen. 3:22), that is, like God, in whose likeness he strove to be formed by following the means the devil proposed to him and taught.

Thus, by disobedience and rebellion he became with the devil the most miserable of all creatures, together with the entire human race, and would have been left in this miserable state had not God by His mercy rescued him.

TIMOTHY: You have now explained this to me better than I understood it previously. Therefore I see a little more clearly and further than I had before. Firstly, besides the disobedience and contempt of the majesty of God and the sacrilege against the divine honor which was Adam and Eve's sin, I consider also that God was even more greatly dishonored because these two both committed this dishonor by placing more faith in the devil's word than in His.

DANIEL: What you say is the same as considering God (who is goodness itself contrary to all envy, and the infallible Truth) an envious man and a liar, and to regard the devil as good and true. Isn't this the same as placing God in the position of the devil and the devil in the place of God?

TIMOTHY: Indeed, it truly is.

HOW ALMOST ALL THE SINS OF MAN CONTAIN ALL THE OFFENSES INCLUDED IN ADAM'S SIN; AND HOW THEY FOLLOW IN ITS NATURE

DANIEL: If you also closely consider the nature of all sins which man ordinarily commits, you will find the very same offenses and crimes within them. For, firstly, there is no sin whatever, no matter how small we might consider it, which does not bear with it disobedience against God, and even against His divine majesty.

Secondly, why is it that man prefers to follow the ways of the devil rather than the ways and calling of God? Isn't it because the path they take and their own counsel seems to them to better provide for their affairs than God's counsel? And whenever and as often as these men set themselves against the Word of God, isn't their counsel the same as the counsel of the devil? And how is their understanding and wisdom any different than that of the devil in which Adam and Eve sought to be instructed, forsaking God's wisdom in which they were firstly instructed (in which wisdom they would always have remained prudent and wise with a true knowledge and a divine wisdom if they had contented themselves with having God their Creator as their sole Master without placing themselves in the school of the devil)?

TIMOTHY: You now mention an evil more common among men than anything else, and which resides chiefly in the most knowledgeable and wisest in the world. For, whatever God has declared, spoken, taught, demonstrated, and commanded in His Word, must then be censored by men who add, subtract, change, or wholly reverse all that He declared and set forth as if they possessed sounder advice or some better counsel than He does and were thereby more knowing, wiser, and better equipped for all their affairs, and as if they better understood than He Himself how He ought to be served and honored.

DANIEL: What they do in turning from His Word confirms all that you say. Or they act as if they thought that God envied them and that He gave them no good counsel, or that He had badly managed their affairs. This is the true ruin of all and the reason why God so often overturns all human counsels and plans, and why all they do comes to nothing, and why what generally comes to pass is what they fear the most and what they endeavor the most to avoid by their wisdom and counsel, scorning and abandoning the wisdom and counsel of God.

TIMOTHY: It is true.

NINE

Man Seeking to Be God and God Becoming Man

HOW MAN REVERSES THE PURPOSE FOR WHICH HE WAS CREATED, AND HOW HE PLACES HIMSELF IN THE POSITION OF GOD

DANIEL: Also, seeing that God created man and all other creatures for His own glory, there is no doubt that they overthrow the end for which they were created by God when they do not direct to His glory all their thoughts, desires, wills, words, and works. But where will we find those who have this regard and who do not look to man rather than God? Where can we find those who have more care for God's honor and glory than for their own glory and earthly gain?

TIMOTHY: Instead, how many do we see who, far from having more care for the honor of God than their own, they don't even care about it at all and never think of it, but have so forgotten and are so in love with themselves that they would be content if God were cast from His throne and were God no longer, so that they might remain in their greatness or make themselves more grand instead of humbling and abasing themselves to give Him glory and render Him the honor which is His due!

DANIEL: When men set themselves and their own honor, profit, pleasures, and sensual delights as the reason why they were created by God, and not God their Creator and His honor and glory, it is quite evident that they place themselves in the position of God and thus attempt to made themselves god and to depose God from His throne (as much as they are able). Now if a man looks to none but himself and renders to himself what he owes to God, he does not serve God as He alone must be served, but rather himself, and in doing this he openly sets himself in the place of God.

TIMOTHY: What you say is as clear as day, if we would only consider it well. Therefore, seeing that in every sin men render to themselves or other creatures what they must render to God to honor Him, and that they therefore place last what He has commanded so that they can follow their own desires, it clearly follows that they prefer themselves and the creatures rather than God the Creator and esteem Him less than if He had never been their Commander and as if they were never His subjects and as if He had no authority over them. For we render honor and reverence not only to kings and rulers who have lordship over us and can command us, but also to others who possess some majesty and authority and some gift of God greater than we do. For, if they possess no lordship which demands our honor, natural decency compels us to respect them—indeed, even if we have never received more of the Law of God than the law of nature which remains written on the hearts of men from their first creation and birth.

DANIEL: Seeing that it is so, how much more do we owe God in all matters, and what gross insult do we render Him when we prefer ourselves to Him, not only in neglecting to do what He commands us but also in committing what He has forbidden us to do in order that we might serve our own wicked desires instead of serving Him?

TIMOTHY: That is easy to judge.

HOW TYRANTS AND PERSECUTORS OF THE PEOPLE OF GOD MAKE GODS OF THEMSELVES

DANIEL: Now, though all sin has this vice couched within it, yet the Spirit of God most particularly condemns the haughty, the wickedly ambitious, the prideful, and particularly tyrants who despise His majesty and persecute His people and Church. And therefore the Lord through Isaiah reproached the king and tyrant of Babylon, saying: "For thou hast said in thine heart, I will ascend into heaven, I will exalt my throne above the stars of God: I will sit also upon the mount of the congregation, in the sides of the north: I will ascend above the heights of the clouds; I will be like the most High" (Isa. 14:13-14). We needn't think that there was ever a ruler, king, or tyrant who literally attempted such a thing or who even thought it possible to accomplish the words of the prophet according to how they literally sound. Nevertheless, the prophet and the Spirit of God who speaks by him never lie.

And therefore we must understand that, though tyrants are compelled—whether they like it or not—to recognize that they are mortal men and that there exists some divinity or at least some greater power than theirs, yet they so intoxicate themselves by their ambition, pride, and prosperity that it appears that they have forgotten everything and that they make themselves believe that they are gods themselves and that there is neither God nor divinity nor power whatever who might resist and hinder their schemes.

Secondly, they show by their endeavors and efforts that they acknowledge no other god in heaven besides their own arm, authority, power, and strength. And therefore when they speak, they speak not as mortal men, but as immortal gods possessing all power, which none can disobey. For they are not accustomed to say "I will say or do this or that if it pleases God," but rather "I will say, I will do, and no one can forbid me." Indeed, they often accompany these words with horrible blasphemies and defiance against God.

Also, when they attack the people of God in an attempt to destroy and ruin them and hinder the course of the Gospel, they do all just as though they attempted to cast God from His throne and establish themselves in His place. For, seeing that God is the support of His people and the foundation upon which His house the Church is founded, they must indeed think that they cannot cast God down (who is the foundation and support) unless they also cast down what is founded and upheld by Him. But, seeing that God promised His Church that He would be their everlasting protection and that she would be eternal, they will not make God a liar (as they seek to do), as though He were neither God nor truthful in His words. Thus it is not surprising that the Spirit of God speaks this language to better display the arrogance and presumption which is natural to men and which lurks in their heart, particularly those who surpass others in authority, power, and earthly prosperity.

This is why the prophet Ezekiel uses words with the king of Tyre similar to what Isaiah said to the king of Babylon (Eze. 28:1-6). Also, when God employs these tyrants as His scourges, they ascribe to their own understanding, wisdom, power, force, and strength all that God does by them, as is shown by Sennacherib, Nebuchadnezzar, and other similar rulers.

TIMOTHY: It is not surprising if tyrants, who have no true understanding or true fear of God, give themselves such glory. For there are very few indeed even of those who have received the most gifts and graces of God who recognize them as they ought to and who do not cease to endlessly steal from God at least some portion of His glory. For, even in giving glory to God for what He has made us, we often retain something by which we also in some way seek our own glory.

DANIEL: If the best and the most perfect men themselves cannot entirely avoid this vice of always stealing some small portion from Him instead of giving and rendering to God all the honor He requires of us and which is His due, how must it be with those who have entirely forgotten God? You can thus understand how even the most just and most perfect still forget themselves so much as to desire to be gods, or equal with Him, and ascribe to themselves all—or at least part—of the honor and glory due to Him alone.

TIMOTHY: The worst of it is that all men still do as you say, and do not guard themselves against it.

DANIEL: This is the reason why they do not understand the heinousness and great depravity of their sins as they ought. And because of this they cannot understand the punishment they deserve.

TIMOTHY: What a great evil it is that we recognize this so poorly and that we take so little thought of God and His majesty!

THE PENALTY WHICH THE SINS OF MAN DESERVE; AND THE WRATH OF GOD REVEALED AGAINST THEM IN THE DEATH OF JESUS CHRIST; AND THE MEANS TO BE DELIVERED FROM THEM; AND IN WHAT SENSE WE MUST UNDERSTAND THAT GOD CREATED NO MAN TO DAMN HIM

DANIEL: Therefore, if God punished with eternal death all mankind who had ever been, are, or yet shall be, He would do them no wrong but would have judged righteously. Therefore the fact that He saves those who flee to His mercy proceeds from His pure grace alone, by which indeed He declares to us what punishment we have merited. For, seeing that it was necessary for His own Son to bear the penalty due the sins of those to whom He willed to show His grace, He clearly displayed by this that there was no punishment whatever which could satisfy His judgment except that of His Son, who because of His great innocence, righteousness, and perfect obedience, was alone sufficient for such a satisfaction. For, if man could bear such a punishment by which he could satisfy the eternal justice of God, there would be no hell or eternal damnation, for the punishments would one day end. But because they shall never have an end, they declare that they are not sufficient for such a satisfaction.

Secondly, because the punishments cannot be sufficient, they must be eternal, except for those who have received Jesus Christ by faith, who bore the wrath of God and the punishments due their sins in order to deliver them, as it is written: "He that believeth on the Son hath everlasting life: and he that believeth not the Son shall not see life; but the wrath of God abideth on him" (John 3:36).

And, concerning what you said about God creating none to damn them, I agree with this statement (if it is properly understood), but not in the sense that those take it who claim this point to abuse the grace and goodness of God.

It is very true that God created no man with the sole purpose of damning him, for "the Lord hath made all things for Himself: yea, even the wicked for the day of evil," as we already discussed (Prov. 16:4). This is the chief end of all the works of God. Yet He does not cease to damn and punish with eternal death those who scorn and despise His Law and His holy Word; so their damnation serves to His glory, which is why they were created. For His glory lies not only in showing mercy to His own but also in showing judgment, by which He reveals His justice against His enemies.

Let us then beware of toying with Him and deceiving ourselves. For, though by His great power and wisdom He is able to derive good from the evil that the wicked commit and is able to turn it to serve for His own honor and glory and for the salvation of His elect (instead of the wicked turning His good creatures and works to evil), yet He never ceases to hate the evil as much as it is evil and the abuse of His creatures and His gifts and graces, and to condemn and punish those who commit such crimes, if they do not receive their remission by His grace and mercy in Jesus Christ.

HOW ALL SIN IS DAMNABLE BY NATURE AND YET IT CANNOT DAMN BELIEVERS

TIMOTHY: From what I understand by your words, it seems to me that you conclude that all sins are damnable to all the unbelieving and reprobates, but that the elect of God and believers are able to receive pardon for them.

DANIEL: It is quite certain that there is no sin whatever which of its nature is worthy of pardon and which is insufficient to damn someone. But if you understand by *damnable* the sin which damns, and by the other that which receives pardon, it is quite clear that in this sense there is no sin which can damn the elect and faithful and which cannot be pardoned by the merit and satisfaction of Jesus Christ. For this reason Paul says: "There is therefore now no condemnation to them which are in Christ Jesus, who walk not after the flesh, but after the Spirit" (Rom. 8:1).

TIMOTHY: Then those who believe in Jesus Christ are blessed.

DANIEL: There are no others blessed besides these. Therefore David says: "Blessed is he whose transgression is forgiven, whose sin is covered. Blessed is the man unto whom the LORD imputeth not iniquity" (Psa. 32:1-2). He does not call blessed the man who finds himself without sin, for there are none, nor ever were, nor ever shall be, except Jesus Christ, truly God and truly man. But he calls blessed the man who, though he is a sinner, has yet found grace and pardon from his sin before God.

However, if we wish to be partakers of this blessedness, we must beware of abusing this grace of God granted to us in Jesus Christ. For, if we do so, instead of rendering our sins pardonable, we shall instead render them doubly damning.

TEN

The Hardening Nature of Sin

THE MEANS WHICH MUST BE TAKEN TO COMBAT SIN AND RESIST IT; AND THE FEAR WE MUST HAVE OF BECOMING HARDENED IN IT

TIMOTHY: Tell me then what remedy we must seek to avoid this great evil.

DANIEL: If we walk by the Spirit and not by the flesh, the very instant our evil desire pricks us, we must resist it by the Spirit of God. If we do not resist it, this is a sign that the Spirit of God is not dwelling within us, which is a characteristic of unbelievers, who follow their evil desire with unrestraint with no fear of God.

If we do resist and yet our sinful heart and weakness overcome us, the next remedy is to prevent our evil will from proceeding any further.

If the violence of the evil will and our own infirmity is so great that we proceed as far as the outward act itself, the other nearest remedy is to not make an occupation of it and to neither return to nor continue in it, and to correct by true repentance all such offenses, both internal and external, and to truly amend them.

If it happens that we occasionally fall again, we must beware of lulling ourselves to sleep and of continuing so far that God abandons us and hardens our hearts and "(gives us) over to a reprobate mind" (Rom. 1:28), to punish our ingratitude and perversity, so that we finally proceed as far as to resist the Spirit of God and that, being convinced by it in our heart, we come to blaspheme Him, as often happens to those who despise and scorn the warnings which are made to them and the reproofs of their own conscience and who rest assured even in their own wickedness (Rom. 9:33). Such a sin can have no forgiveness and is called by John the "sin unto death" (1 John 5:16; Matt. 12:31-32). Therefore he who sins against the Holy Spirit rejects Him without whom he can neither call for nor obtain pardon or be made a partaker of Jesus Christ, who alone is our Life and Salvation (1 Cor. 12:13; Rom. 8:9).

Let us then beware of following the example of Cain, Pharaoh, Saul, Judas, and the scribes and Pharisees who remained hardened and obstinate in their sins (Gen. 4:1-10; Ex. 8:15, 32; 9:35; 1 Sam. 15:24-35; Matt. 26:47-50, 59-60; Rom. 9:17). But let us instead follow the example of David, the sinful woman, Peter, Paul, and other similar servants of God who recognized and forsook their offenses and returned to God with all their hearts (Psa. 51:1-4; Matt. 26:73-75; Luke 7:37-50; 1 Tim. 1:13-16).

SINS COMMITTED BY SIMPLE IGNORANCE OR WEAKNESS AND THOSE COMMITTED WITH CAREFUL DELIBERATION; AND THE SINS OF PETER, JUDAS, AND DAVID TO THIS SAME PURPOSE

TIMOTHY: This warning and admonition is well worthy of note. I will now ask you what you understand by the sin against the Holy Spirit, if you have not already said it. But it reminds me of what you said when we spoke of the persecutors who persecute the Gospel by a deliberate wickedness and an intentional scorning of God like the devil, against their own conscience and the power of the Spirit of God which they have already tasted and felt and by which they were convinced in their hearts.

I had formerly thought that all those who sin willfully against the very knowledge they have of the evil they do and of which their conscience rebukes and reproaches them had sinned against the Holy Spirit. But now I clearly understand that if this were so, there would remain few indeed who had not at some time sinned against the Holy Spirit. For, by understanding it this way, nearly all sins except those committed in ignorance would be sins against the Holy Spirit.

DANIEL: What you say is true, except that we might still add to the sins committed in ignorance many other sins committed rather out of sheer weakness than by deliberate intent, like the sin of Peter when he denied Jesus Christ. For he was not unaware that what he did was evil (Matt. 26:69-74). For, when Jesus Christ predicted that he would do it, he there openly opposed it as a very wicked thing, assuring Him and affirming that he would rather die than ever commit such a vile act. By this he truly showed that his conscience recognized that this was a very grave sin, seeing that he acknowledged the same when he confessed with his mouth that he would rather die than commit such an offense. It was thus not a sin committed in ignorance, as Paul testifies of himself that he sinned when he persecuted the Church. For he did not persecute them out of a hatred he bore to the known truth, but instead thought he was doing good and thought he was persecuting the apostates and heretics. However, this in no way excused him from his grievous sin.

But, even though Peter fell so heavily and in such a grievous error, yet it was not done out of malice or some wicked desire or by a conscious, intentional battling against and resisting his own conscience, as Judas, who had the devil within his heart and had so hardened himself that, though Jesus Christ warned him, he was no more moved by that than the devil himself (John 13:21-30; Luke 22:3-6, 21-23). And therefore God did not give him grace (as He did Peter) to recognize his offence with true repentance and hope of pardon, but only with a despair in which he remained sunk and engulfed.

But when Peter denied Jesus Christ—even with oaths and violent curses—he was so surprised and staggered and overcome and distraught with fear and terror that he could not take time to think of what he did or even debate it with his conscience. And therefore he as it were entirely forgot everything he had heard from Jesus Christ and what he had promised Him, and remained in this state as dazed and dumbfounded as though he did not sense his wrong until Jesus Christ looked at him and the cock crowed, as Jesus Christ had predicted (Luke 22:55-62). Thus a great sin was committed, though it was done by simple weakness of the flesh and not with conscious deliberation.

But the adultery and murder of David is different in its manner than that of Peter, for David was not enticed to do the evil he committed by any allurement except his own wicked desire, and he indeed had time enough to deliberate with his conscience. For he knew quite well that the crimes he committed displeased God, seeing that He had judged them worthy of death in His Law. And he also found himself in no danger of his life (as did Peter), nor was he pressed by others except by his own evil eye of concupiscence with which he gazed on Bathsheba and of the concern he had for his own honor before men more than the honor of God. And therefore he was as it were intoxicated and wholly blinded by his evil desire which had so hypnotized him in his sin that he continued quite some time as if he had wholly forgotten God and His Word and all religion, and indeed even himself, and that he had no fear of God before his eyes.

SINS COMMITTED WITH CONSCIOUS DELIBERATION BY WEAKNESS; AND SINS PROCEEDING FROM UNBELIEF AND A SCORNING OF GOD; AND THE COMPARISON OF DAVID AND SAUL'S SINS IN THIS REGARD

TIMOTHY: If we consider only the outward appearance of these enormous sins of David and those committed by Saul for which God rejected him, and if we compare them with each other, it would seem that Saul was innocent compared to David. For the fact that he sacrificed without waiting for Samuel and kept alive Agag the king of the Amalekites and the fatted bulls and sheep he saved to sacrifice to God can all be covered with the appearance of good intentions. For it truly seems that all this could be made to glorify God and that Saul did it with this intention (1 Sam. 15:9). But we cannot say the same for David, for the sins which he committed are so openly abominable that the wickedest men hold them in abhorrence.

DANIEL: You speak truly. And by the judgment which God made you can know that He doesn't judge sins as man judges, and that He looks more upon the heart than the works. For, as good an exterior as Saul had and as good an appearance and outward show as he made before men, yet his heart never ceased to be wholly filled with unbelief, hypocrisy, and rebellion against God, as was afterward openly revealed. For how many times did his conscience reprove him for the wrong he had shown David—indeed, so much so that he was even constrained to confess this quite clearly and in public, and to condemn himself and justify David? (1 Sam. 24:17-20; 26:21.) And yet he never ceased to pursue him, being as furious and enraged against him as if he judged himself to be innocent and better than he.

Secondly, though he was assuredly warned by Samuel that God had rejected him from the kingdom and had given it to another, nevertheless he sought to reign in contempt of God (1 Sam. 15:26; 28:1-6). And, seeing himself utterly abandoned by God, he personally sought aid from the devil by means of sorcery, though previously he had justly executed those who had been known to be given to such diabolical arts, according to the Law of God. And besides all this we have his despairing death, in which he killed himself by his own sword (1 Sam. 31:4-5). You can thus judge by all this how Saul continuously waged war against his own conscience and against the Spirit of God in such a way that he finally utterly forsook and abandoned God in order to give himself up to the devil.

But David did not do this. Therefore, though he sinned in laying a snare, yet he was overcome more by the weakness of the flesh still remaining within him than by an open rebellion against God and His Law. For, though he was not ignorant of this, yet the evil desire which still remained enrooted in his flesh so troubled his sense and understanding that he was as it were carried outside of himself and then lulled to sleep and buried in his sin until God awakened him by Nathan His prophet.

But, as soon as God announced His judgment by him, he humbled himself with true repentance and confession of his sin and placed himself wholly in the hands of his God, and then patiently received all the beatings and chastisements which it pleased God to send him (2 Sam. 12:1-14).

By this he clearly showed that, though he committed such execrable sins, yet he always possessed a heart more right before God than Saul, according to the testimony God Himself made, saying that He found in him "a man after His own heart" (Acts 13:22). But God permitted him to fall so that all might know what David was according to his own nature and what he was by the grace of God, in order that grace might be better recognized in him and that He might reveal more openly His mercy toward poor sinners. And therefore after David came to himself and obtained grace from God he did not return to his sins or persevere in them as Saul did in his, but to the contrary he lived all the rest of his life in greater humility and in a greater fear of God than ever before.

VARIOUS DEGREES OF IGNORANCE, WEAKNESS, WICKEDNESS, AND OBSTINACY, AND THEIR COMBINATION IN THE SINS OF MEN

TIMOTHY: All these examples greatly assist me in better understanding all that we previously discussed regarding the nature of sin and its various types. For I now see what difference there is between the sins which are made by simple ignorance or by simple weakness and surprise and those which are made by wickedness and laying snares, and against all remonstrances of conscience, and against the Holy Spirit.

DANIEL: You must add to simple ignorance and weakness the sins that are committed by willful and feigned ignorance and weakness. For, when men are willingly ignorant and are content in their ignorance and weakness, not striving against it as they ought, such ignorance and weakness is even more inexcusable. And when men are already so sluggish and hardened in their sins that their conscience is as if wholly exhausted so that they feel no remorse in it, there is little hope of salvation for them. For then they must be placed alongside those of whom Paul speaks in such terms: "This I say therefore, and testify in the Lord, that ye henceforth walk not as other Gentiles walk, in the vanity of their mind, having the understanding darkened, being alienated from the life of God through the ignorance that is in them, because of the blindness of their heart: who being past feeling have given themselves over unto lasciviousness, to work all uncleanness with greediness" (Eph. 4:17-19).

Now, if those who have thus lost all feeling both of God and conscience are in such a miserable and desperate state, what can we hope of those who consciously and deliberately battle against their own conscience, against revealed truth, and against the Spirit of God by which they are convinced in their heart?

TIMOTHY: I think that these are not far from the sin leading to death and the sin against the Holy Spirit of which we previously spoke.

DANIEL: If they have not already fallen, they are at least very near the edge and brink. Therefore they lack but a step or two before they hurl themselves over and are entirely lost. And therefore we must truly beware of passing too closely by them. For, though there is no sin at all proceeding from the natural corruption within us in which ignorance and wickedness are not always joined together, yet the sins which proceed more from wickedness than ignorance are much graver than those which proceed more from ignorance than wickedness. Seeing it is so, you can easily see why these are so much more heinous, from the amount of utmost wickedness within them against the knowledge of God, by which the ignorance appears small indeed in comparison to the wickedness.

TIMOTHY: Give me some examples of these differing degrees of sin.

DANIEL: When Paul persecuted the Christians he did it more out of ignorance than wickedness (Rom. 10:1-3). We can say the same of the other Jews of whom Paul testifies that "they have a zeal of God, but not according to knowledge," and of those for whom Jesus Christ and Stephen prayed in their death, saying: "Father, forgive them; for they know not what they do," and: "Lord, lay not this sin to their charge" (Rom. 10:2; Luke 23:34; Acts 7:60).

But we cannot say the same of many of the scribes and

Pharisees, and of Annas and Caiaphas and the council of Jews who condemned Jesus Christ. For they clearly displayed what spirit they were of, particularly after the death and resurrection of Jesus Christ. For, though they were informed by the guards themselves (who were delegated by them to guard the tomb) of what happened in His resurrection, yet they were not led to repentance by this, but to the contrary they bribed the guards by money—against their own conscience—to make them lie against the truth which they themselves had borne witness to, in order to conceal the resurrection of Jesus Christ. You cannot help but see here an obvious wickedness and perversity which induced them to continually resist God and their own conscience.

TIMOTHY: I see this clearly. May it please God that the same be not found today among those who resist and persecute the Gospel!

DANIEL: You thus see many whom God fully abandoned, giving them over to "a reprobate mind" such that, just as much as they suppressed the truth, so much did they harden their hearts (Rom. 1:28). Therefore we can truly say that the prophecy of Isaiah is accomplished in them, who said: "Shut their eyes, lest they see with their eyes, and hear with their ears, and understand with their heart, and convert, and be healed" (Isa. 6:10).

TIMOTHY: This is a terrible judgment of God, and greatly to be feared.

DANIEL: More so than death.

TIMOTHY: I am now well content and satisfied on all the matters we have discussed, by which I understand the differing degrees of sins and how God judges them, and how necessary it is for us to understand His Law, and that by our free will we can truly damn and lose ourselves, but that it is God alone who can save us by His grace and mercy.

ELEVEN

The First Commandment of the Law

"Thou shalt have no other gods before Me."
— Exodus 20:2

TIMOTHY: The matters we previously dealt with appear very necessary for the general understanding of all the Law of God and its use. I would now like to hear in particular and in detail the explanation of each of the commandments contained in it—that is, the true sense of each of them and in what way they are to be kept or transgressed.

You have already explained the preface and have shown me how we must understand the Law according to the nature and majesty of the Lawgiver, who is God, and how He has divided and comprised the Law into two tables, which contain ten commandments in all; of which the first Table contains those which deal particularly and directly with the majesty of God alone and the honor due Him which He requires before all else, and the other contains what God requires of us toward our neighbor. It now remains for us to enter into the explanation of the first commandment of the first Table.

DANIEL: To better understand it, we must truly consider all the words by which it is set forth to us. It is thus fitting in the first place to know what a *strange* or *other god* is.

Secondly, we must know what it means to have *other* or *strange gods.*

Thirdly, what it is to have them *before the Lord,* and why this is expressly added.

Fourthly, why He used the affirmative instead of the negative, and why He didn't command: "Have Me as your God," but instead forbids us from having any others.

Fifthly, why He spoke in the singular instead of in the plural, as though He only addressed His word to one man and not to many (seeing that this Law is addressed to all), and why He spoke in the second person.

THE UNITY OF GOD AND THE WITNESSES TO IT IN HOLY SCRIPTURE; AND THE PLURALITY OF FALSE AND STRANGE GODS

TIMOTHY: These are very good points and are well worthy of consideration. Following then the order which you have set forth, tell me what a *strange* or *other god* is. I am well assured by Holy Scripture—and firmly believe it, as we render testimony every day by the confession of our faith—that there is only one God and that there can be no other, for a plurality of gods abolishes all deity.

DANIEL: You touch upon an astonishing point and one well worth considering seeing that, instead of being like other things which are increased by multiplication, God is diminished by it. For if you add to one, two, or three, it will grow accordingly and will always increase more and more the more you multiply. It was said of man: "It is not good that the man should be alone; I will make him an help meet for him" (Gen. 2:18).

But it is the opposite with God, for He cannot be such as was previously described if He is not alone. For either He does not exist at all, or He is one only. This is because God cannot be God if He is not sovereign over all, Lord of all things, all powerful, all knowing, wholly good, and wholly perfect, having no lack of anything at all, but to the contrary is sufficient in Himself and is the sufficiency of every creature; having His being in Himself, deriving nothing from any other, but giving being to all things that have ever been, are, or ever shall be.

For, if He were many gods, they could not all be

sovereign, but would be equals. Likewise they could not all be all powerful, all knowing, wholly good, wholly perfect, having their being and sufficiency in themselves, and giving being to others. For it would always necessarily ensue that some would possess something of the others and that none among them would be the sole possessor of all things, and thus could not be God. For whoever gives God an equal denies that there is a God.

And therefore it is written: "Hear, O Israel: the Lord our God is one Lord" (Deut. 6:4). This is as much as to say "He alone is God," and thus it is translated in the French Bibles. And again: "Unto thee it was shewed, that thou mightest know that the Lord He is God; there is none else beside Him" (Deut. 4:35). And in another place: "So the Lord alone did lead him, and there was no strange god with Him" (Deut. 32:12). And in Joshua: "the Lord your God, He is God in heaven above, and in earth beneath" (Jos. 2:11). And in Malachi: "hath not one God created us?" (Mal. 2:10.) And in the Psalms: "For who is God save the Lord? or who is a rock save our God?" (Psa. 18:31.) And in Paul: "one Lord, one faith, one baptism, one God and Father of all, who is above all, and through all, and in you all" (Eph. 4:5-6). He even concludes with the unity of God, the unity of the Mediator, saying: "there is one God, and one Mediator between God and men, the Man Christ Jesus, who gave Himself a ransom for all" (1 Tim. 2:5-6). And in another place God expressly states by Moses: "See now that I, even I, am He, and there is no god with Me" (Deut. 32:39).

TIMOTHY: That certainly seems to settle it. But, if this is so, why then does He say: "Thou shalt have no other gods before Me"? For, if there is only one God, what other gods can we have?

THE VARIOUS MEANINGS OF THE NAME "GOD" IN HOLY SCRIPTURE, AND THE VARIOUS SENSES IN WHICH IT IS TAKEN, AND IN WHAT WAYS IT IS ATTRIBUTED TO CREATED BEINGS

DANIEL: To properly understand this matter and to fully resolve this difficulty, we must first consider in what ways the name *God* is used in Holy Scripture and to whom it is ascribed and in what sense and in what manner it is used. When it is taken in its proper sense and in its proper meaning, we understand by it the true God, Creator of all things, of whom we have just spoken, who is truly so in both name and reality. But sometimes this name is also ascribed to the creatures, and this is done in two ways. For it is sometimes given by comparison and similarity and sometimes according to the opinions, ways, and customs of men. And in neither of these cases is it taken in its literal meaning.

IN WHAT MANNER THE NAME OF GOD IS ATTRIBUTED TO THE CREATURES BY SIMILARITY AND COMPARISON

TIMOTHY: Explain this to me a little more clearly by examples, if you can.

DANIEL: It is quite simple. First, when the name *god* is ascribed to the creatures because of the similarity and the affinity and likeness that such creatures share with their Creator, it means as much as the word *divine* means in our language when we use it, not as when we call magicians and sorcerers *diviners* who mingle and disclose and make known secret and hidden things and predict things to come by witchcraft, but as we use it when we speak of divine things, understanding by it heavenly and eternal things which are more than human and natural and which more nearly approach the nature of God.

Now we find in Holy Scripture this name attributed in this sense first to the angels and then to men excellent in virtue, wisdom, dignity, and power, as are firstly the true prophets and apostles and all true ministers of God and His Word, and then kings, princes, lords, magistrates, ministers of justice, and all shepherds who have charge and government of the people, and consequently all those who are truly the people of God.

As I said, men excellent in virtue and dignity are called *gods* for nearly the same reason. And, as much as each of them more closely approaches this perfection of understanding, wisdom, power, virtue, goodness, and holiness in God and more closely represents the image of God in himself, he is always rendered more worthy of this name *god,* and declares himself to be truly a godly man, who is like a god in comparison to others.

It is taken in this sense when Moses is called Pharaoh's god and Aaron his brother (Ex. 4:16), and when it is said in the Law: "Thou shalt not revile the gods, nor curse the ruler of thy people," which is speaking of the judges, governors, magistrates, pastors, and protectors (Ex. 22:28; Acts 23:5). Also: "God standeth in the congregation of the mighty; He judgeth among the gods. . . . I have said, Ye are gods; and all of you are children of the Most High. But ye shall die like men, and fall like one of the princes" (Psa. 82:1, 6-7). And our Lord Jesus Christ, explaining these passages, says: "If He called them gods, unto whom the word of God came, and the Scripture cannot be broken; say ye of Him, whom the Father hath sanctified and sent into the world, Thou blasphemest, because I said, I am the Son of God?" (John 10:35-36.)

HOW THE SERVANTS OF GOD TO WHOM THE NAME "GOD" IS ATTRIBUTED ARE NOT INCLUDED AMONG FALSE GODS; AND HOW THIS COMMANDMENT DOES NOT FORBID US TO RENDER THEM THE HONOR DUE THEM

TIMOTHY: Seeing that the Word of God gives this honor to them by communicating to them the name of God, we must not consider them false gods.

DANIEL: It is certain that as long as such people so fulfill their office that they show themselves worthy of such a name, and as long as men consider them as what they are and recognize them as such gods as the Holy Scripture sets forth to us and in such a sense, and do not give them the honor due the only true God but only that which pertains to them by His command, so they must not be considered false gods. Instead we ought to desire that the whole earth were full of such gods, and we should all strive and labor to be of their number. For God is in no way jealous of such gods, but to the contrary He takes great pleasure in them, seeing that the chief reason why He sent Jesus Christ into the world was that by this means we might "become the sons of God" by receiving Him, as John witnesses, which we are by faith in Him

(John 1:12).

But if we abuse the gifts and graces which God has bestowed either upon us or upon others, and ascribe either to ourselves or to any other creature the honor due to God alone, by such an abuse we make false gods of ourselves and of the creatures whom we misuse.

TWELVE

Worshiping God as God

THE HONOR GOD REQUIRES OF US IN HIS LAW; AND THE MAIN POINTS UNDERSTOOD IN ALL DIVINE WORSHIP AND THE CHRISTIAN RELIGION

TIMOTHY: Then, to better understand the manner in which false gods are made, it seems to me that it is still necessary for us to understand better what honor is properly due to God, which cannot be given to any other but Him alone.

DANIEL: It is true. For, if we know this, we will understand the full meaning of this first commandment and all that God requires of us by it.

TIMOTHY: I ask then that you give me your opinion according to the Word of God, for we cannot have the true understanding of such things without it.

DANIEL: It seems to me that we can quite easily summarize all that is treated so fully in Holy Scripture of the honor due to God alone into four main points, into which all others can be included.

TIMOTHY: What is the first?

DANIEL: It is the confidence and trust of our hearts in Him.

TIMOTHY: The next?

DANIEL: Worship.

TIMOTHY: The third?

DANIEL: Invocation, or calling upon God (under which, or likewise under worship, I include thanksgiving).

TIMOTHY: And the fourth?

DANIEL: The obedience and service of the conscience. From these points follow all the true knowledge of God which is the first foundation and the first step by which it is fitting to begin this Law. For the affection of the heart (if it is true) immediately embraces and follows this knowledge. Therefore this is the first thing that the Lord presents to us, both in the preface of His Law and in this first commandment, which is the foundation of all the following commandments.

THE FAITH AND TRUST WE MUST HAVE IN GOD; AND THE REASONS WHY; AND THE HONOR THAT WE RENDER HIM BY IT; AND THE DISHONOR THAT IS PAID HIM BY OUR DISTRUST AND UNBELIEF

TIMOTHY: What do you mean by this trust which you set in the first place?

DANIEL: That we place all our heart in Him in such a way that we await all good from Him and hope for nothing from any other source whatever, but only from Him alone. For we cannot do the contrary without greatly dishonoring Him in many ways.

TIMOTHY: Why?

DANIEL: Because if we do not fully trust in and rely on Him, we do not believe Him to be the Creator of all things, all powerful, all wise, all good, wholly perfect, and the source and perfection of all good, and that none of this exists in anyone else besides Him alone, and by Him, seeing that "in Him we live, and move, and have our being" (Acts 17:28), and are of Him alone, for we "were made by Him; and without Him was not anything made that was made" (John 1:1-4). Now, if we do not regard Him as such, we do not acknowledge Him as true God. For, as we have already said, He cannot truly be God if He is not all these things. Therefore those who cannot endure this and who are driven to despair, like Saul, Judas, and others like them, sin against this commandment, seeing that they do not have this trust in God which is required by it.

But when we trust wholly in Him, we give Him the honor which is His due. For, first, we testify that He is steadfast and true, which no other can be but He alone who has His being in Himself and from whom all creatures derive their own. For all who have a beginning and end cannot always have been and be, and cannot be certain, steadfast, constant, and immutable. For such a one cannot be master or have power of himself, but must always remain subject under the power (and consequently under the will) of others. This cannot be so in God, seeing that He has no superior and can undergo no change whatever.

For, as Moses says: "God is not a man, that He should lie; neither the son of man, that He should repent" (Num. 23:19). And therefore He Himself says by Malachi: "I am the LORD, I change not" (Mal. 3:6). And in Isaiah and Revelation: "I am the First, and I am the Last" (Isa. 44:6; Rev. 1:8; 21:6; 22:13). It is likewise written that He is always in the same state and that all things "shall perish; . . . and they shall all wax old," and that "all men are liars," but He is "the same, and [His] years shall have no end," nor shall He perish or grow old (Heb. 1:11; Psa. 116:11; 102:26).

By trusting in Him we acknowledge Him as all powerful, all wise, all good, and wholly perfect. For we declare firstly that we hold it as certain that He indeed possesses the power to do what we hope from Him. Secondly, that He possesses the wisdom to know how to guide our affairs, and also the will to instantly do so—indeed, in such a manner that nothing further shall ever be desired for His glory and our salvation.

Secondly, no creature whatever could in any way hinder Him from accomplishing—without the least difficulty—all that

He pleases both in heaven and in earth, and nothing can please Him unless it is wholly good and to our great benefit.

THE HAPPINESS OF THE MAN WHO PLACES HIS TRUST IN GOD; AND THE FIRM SUPPORT WHICH HE HAS IN HIM; AND HOW THERE IS NOTHING IN MAN UPON WHICH WE MIGHT SECURELY FOUND OUR SUPPORT AND TRUST; AND HOW WE MAKE FALSE GODS OF CREATURES IN WHOM WE PLACE OUR TRUST

TIMOTHY: Seeing then that the true God has all things in Himself, we can and must trust in Him indeed. For whoever possesses these things cannot be unfaithful to those who trust in Him.

DANIEL: And therefore it is said and repeated so many times in Holy Scripture that those are blessed who place their trust in Him and that they are steadfast and cannot ever be shaken or moved. Hence David says: "The Lord is my rock, and my fortress, and my deliverer; my God, my strength, in whom I will trust; . . . In God is my salvation and glory: the rock of my strength, and my refuge, is in God" (Psa. 18:2; 62:7).

On the other hand, whoever does not have these things within himself cannot fail to be unfaithful to himself and to all those who place their trust in him; as we daily experience in ourselves. For how many times do we change our mind and act utterly contrary to what we undertook and promised? This happens to us either by constraint or because the ability fails us or by our own decision because of our evil will or because we know that we have been deceived by a lack of prudence and wisdom. If it so happens that we are daily unfaithful to ourselves, is it any marvel that we are unfaithful to others and that others are also often unfaithful to us?

TIMOTHY: I am not surprised that this is the case. We instead have much more reason to be astonished when the creatures are *not* unfaithful to us.

DANIEL: And therefore I conclude that this commandment

requires of us all that Holy Scripture deals with regarding the faith and trust we owe to God alone, and that every man who puts this faith and trust in any creature at all is an idolater and creates for himself a false god from the creature in whom he places such trust.

THE DIFFERENCE BETWEEN THE TRUST THAT WE MUST HAVE IN GOD AND THAT WHICH WE CAN HAVE IN MEN AND THE CREATURES; AND HOW WE CAN TRUST OURSELVES TO THE CREATURES IN GOD; AND THE FOUNDATION OF OUR TRUST IN HIM

TIMOTHY: It thus follows from what you say that we must not place our trust in any person at all. But this is something not only strongly contrary to the nature of Christian love, which (as Paul testifies), "thinketh no evil, . . . believeth all things, hopeth all things," but would also be a great torment and a true hell in human society and in the dealings which men must have with one another (1 Cor. 13:5, 7). For where would we be if we dared not trust anyone? We would never be in peace, but always in fear. And consequently our life would be more miserable than that of tyrants who live in perpetual fear because they dare not trust anyone, or of those who are under their tyranny who cannot live under them without fear.

DANIEL: I grant you this. Therefore do not think by my explanation that I wish to abolish the faith and trust which we must render to each other, without which the human race could not be maintained or preserved. To the contrary, I wish rather to establish it. Hence what I say is intended only to show the difference which must exist between the faith and trust we owe to God and that which we owe to men and other creatures. For I must trust in God as He alone who can know me and desires of Himself to do the good which I hope to receive from Him.

In this way I cannot trust in man or in any creature whatever, not even in the angels themselves, for they are not such as He is. Therefore I cannot entrust myself to them except inasmuch as I wait on God for what it might please Him to grant me in goods or blessings by their ministry. Then, trusting in the creature in this regard, I would not properly be trusting in the creature but in God our Creator; indeed, in such a way that I take as assured the fact that God Himself, despite them, will grant me by them the good which He knows is necessary for me and that He will turn to good the evil which they wish to do me, as often happens. For many often do us good, not seeking however to do so, but thinking rather to do us harm.

Thus, seeing that every creature is under the power of God, when God promises me aid by someone, I must completely trust this creature that I will receive the good that God promised me in him and from him, for my trust is then founded on God and on His Word and not on the creature. But if I base my trust on no more than the promise of the creature or on the opinion and expectation which I have imagined in myself, my trust is not assured. Therefore all trust that I place in the creature by any other condition than what has been said is pure idolatry, and this creature is to me a false god.

But, in the trust which I must place in God, there is no other condition except His will alone, of which we are assured by His promises. For, just as I wait on God in vain for what He has not promised me, so also I cannot be deprived of what He has promised. For He is not subject to my whims or constrained to give me what I please, but He will give me what He is pleased in His pure goodness and grace to give me and what He has declared by His Word to be pleasing to Him. Faith looks to this Word, without which it cannot be faith but is instead mere whim, fancy, and opinion. And therefore He says: "Hear, O My people, and I will testify unto thee: O Israel, if thou wilt hearken unto Me; there shall no strange god be in thee; neither shalt thou worship any strange god" (Psa. 81:8-9).

HOW THE TRUST IN GOD REQUIRED BY THIS FIRST COMMANDMENT INCLUDES ALL THE TEACHING BY WHICH GOD HAS REVEALED HIMSELF TO MEN

TIMOTHY: It follows then from this that the faith which is the first fruit of the true knowledge of God, which is set forth for us in this commandment, includes the knowledge of His Word and a consent to it, by which we approve and receive as true and certain all that is revealed to us of Him in it—that is, all the articles of our faith and all the promises and curses which are contained within it.

DANIEL: It is just as you say. Therefore we must diligently note what we have already heard in the preface to this Law: "I am the Lord thy God, which have brought thee out," etc. For, in speaking like this, God clearly declares by these words that He cares for you and that it is He who calls you, who gives you His Word, who reveals Himself to you, who gives you a testimony of His presence and favor, and who will aid you, answer you, and save you, both in this life and in that which is to come. But, above all, it is well worth noting that He said "*thy* God." For He declares by this word that He has covenanted with the people to whom He thus speaks and that He has a covenant with no other but only with him who hears His Word, and that He receives for His Church none among men except those who hear and receive this Word.

And faith in this Word immediately follows the true fear of God and true love, hope, humility, and patience, as we will explain more fully afterward. For, because faith looks to the curses that God makes against sinners, it teaches us to recognize what punishments we have merited from Him and also teaches us to fear and patiently bear His rod as just and righteous. Furthermore, when faith regards His promises, it teaches us to love and to place our hope in Him—even in death itself—and to commit all things to His good will.

THIRTEEN

False Gods and the Gods of Scripture

HOW MEN CREATE FALSE GODS BY THE TRUST THEY PLACE IN CREATURES; AND HOW THEY ARE WITHOUT GOD; AND HOW BY THIS MEANS THEY HONOR THE DEVIL INSTEAD OF GOD

TIMOTHY: Seeing then that faith and trust in God is one of the main points of the honor we owe Him and which He requires of us and is like the foundation of all others, I now clearly understand by what you have said that whoever places this faith and trust in any other than in God creates for himself and makes as many new and false gods as there are creatures in which he places this faith and trust.

DANIEL: The reason is very clear. For, seeing that he attributes to them what is reserved to God, he places them in the position of God, and in this way they become gods to him according to his whim and desire. Thus this is another way in which men make for themselves false gods, which are however no gods at all except by the error, abuse, and conceit of their own understanding. For it is not in the power of man to make gods. And therefore it is written: "the gods of the nations are idols" (Psa. 96:5). Therefore they are not gods. Some translators translate this passage thus: "the gods of the Gentiles are demons." And idols, not without good cause, can indeed be called demons. For, as soon as we ascribe to others the honor due to God, we receive the devil in the place of God. For no creature desires to strip from God the honor due Him alone in order to ascribe it to himself except the devil and those men led by his spirit. Therefore all such fantasy and desire by which such gods are forged proceeds from the devil and his school, his workshop, and is linked to him.

Therefore Paul calls him "the god of this world [who] hath blinded the minds of them which believe not" (2 Cor. 4:4). And, speaking of the gods fashioned in the workshop of this cursed god who is the creator of all false and strange gods, he says: "we know that an idol is nothing in the world, and that there is none other God but one. For though there be that are called gods, whether in heaven or in earth, (as there be gods many, and lords many,) but to us there is but one God, the Father, of whom are all things, and we in Him; and one Lord Jesus Christ, by whom are all things, and we by Him" (1 Cor. 8:4-6). This is why he calls the Gentiles, who had such gods for their gods, men "without God" (Eph. 2:12).

WHY THE NAME OF GOD IS ATTRIBUTED TO THOSE WHO ARE NOT GODS; AND WHAT TEACHING IS PROPOSED TO THE RULERS AND MINISTERS OF GOD WHEN THIS NAME IS GIVEN THEM; AND HOW THEY CAN BE MADE FALSE GODS

TIMOTHY: We can already understand by this how many false gods man can create in this way alone. He can make as many as there are creatures both in heaven and on earth. But, seeing that such gods who are called by this name by likeness and similarity and by the error of human understanding are not gods at all, why is this title given to them in the Holy Scriptures?

DANIEL: This is not done without reason. When angels and great men are called gods, the Holy Scripture teaches us many things at once by this. The first is that the creatures who are called by this name must recognize what they are, seeing that the honor which is attributed to them proceeds from Him whose name they bear. They must bear this in mind so that they don't ascribe the honor to themselves, but to God alone, from whom they derive all that they have.

The other is that those who bear such names are

admonished by this to wholly conform themselves to the image of Him whose name is given them in order that they might employ the power, wisdom, and all the gifts they have received from Him to serve for His glory and for the good of all those who are under their charge, as an example of Him whom they represent. If they do the contrary and set themselves in the place of God, ascribing to themselves what they have received from Him and what God has done through them, seeking to have men obey them rather than Him and demanding the honors which are due Him by seeking to keep them for themselves and abusing their power by tyranny and changing their wisdom into guile and wickedness, being like a plague on those whose wellbeing they ought to procure, then they make themselves strange gods and greatly dishonor God.

For, just as we do not recognize strangers and do not receive them as we do our friends and family, so also God does not recognize as His servants those who abuse their office against His honor, but to the contrary He disowns and rejects them as strangers and enemies. Pharaoh, Sennacherib, Nebuchadnezzar, the king of Tyre, Herod, and others like them who are mentioned in the Holy Scriptures and likewise many emperors, kings, rulers, lords, and other great men who were among the pagans have turned themselves into false gods in this way by their impudence, pride, arrogance, presumption, tyranny, and love of themselves, and by the assurance and confidence in their own power, despising God and His providence. For all these vices are contrary to this commandment, seeing that they are wholly contrary to the fear of God required in it.

HOW THE POPE AND HIS PROPHETS ARE MADE STRANGE GODS, AND BY WHOM

TIMOTHY: And can't the pope and his adherents also be placed in this category?

DANIEL: Who indeed deserves this more than "the son of perdition; who opposeth and exalteth himself above all that is called God, or that is worshipped; so that he as God sitteth in the temple of God, shewing himself that he is God"? (2 Thes. 2:3-4.) We can also include with him all his false prophets and all the tyrants joined with them. For when the pope and his adherents by their decrees and canons ascribe to themselves judgment over all, exempting themselves from all judgment and attributing to themselves the power to pardon and retain sins, to open and to close heaven, to save and to damn, to give laws and commandments to bind the conscience, to ordain sacraments by their own authority, and to promise salvation by them and by their ceremonies and traditions, aren't they ascribing to themselves what belongs to God? And don't they require us to place in them and in their laws the faith and trust which we owe to God and to His Word alone?

And those who follow them and who believe in their traditions and seek their own salvation from them, don't they make them into their gods? Haven't they made them strange gods, particularly the tyrants who uphold their own traditions more diligently than the very Word of God and who more grievously punish those who transgress their own laws than those who transgress the entirety of the Law of God? This is nearly the same way in which the Gentiles placed such mortal men in the position of God, by which they have filled heaven and earth with false gods.

THE WARNING GOD GIVES THOSE WHO ARE SUBJECT TO MAGISTRATES AND AUTHORITIES, WHO ARE SHEPHERDS TO WHOM IS ATTRIBUTED THE NAME OF GOD; AND HOW WE CAN MAKE STRANGE GODS BOTH OF THEM, OF ANGELS, AND OF SAINTS; AND THE MEANS THAT MUST BE TAKEN IN ORDER THAT GOD BE NOT DISHONORED IN THEM

TIMOTHY: You have explained the lesson which God gave to rulers, shepherds, and to persons in authority when He imparted His name to them in the Holy Scriptures. But is there nothing further for those who are subject to them?

DANIEL: We must also note on our part that this name of God given to great men admonishes us that we must not think anything of them except what we have said, which they must think of themselves. For, if we do otherwise, though they think no more of themselves than they ought and though they render to God the honor which is His due, nevertheless we make false gods of them if we depend on them as if they derived from themselves what was given them by God and if we place our confidence in them instead of relying on God. In this way we make devils and strange gods of the angels, just as the pagans previously did. We also do the same with saints, just as the pagans did of the men they deified—that is, whom they took for gods.

And therefore it is written: "Put not your trust in princes, nor in the son of man, in whom there is no help" (Psa. 146:3). And, regarding ministers, Paul declares that "though we, or an angel from heaven, preach any other gospel unto you than that which we have preached unto you, let him be accursed" (Gal. 1:8). By this he very clearly shows that we must not believe the Word of God on account of the authority of those who present it. For this would be to trust in the creature—not in God—and to set the creature in His place. But we must believe it because it comes from God—indeed, even if all the angels themselves and all the creatures contradict it. This is also why Jesus Christ forbids us to be "called masters: for one is your Master, even Christ" (Matt. 23:8).

If we do injury to God in this way and make false gods of men when we approve or condemn His Word by the authority of men, how much more do we make them gods when for this sole reason we receive their false teaching as the Word of God? This is not properly understanding why great men are called gods.

And, just as some err in this place, so others also greatly err who do not recognize in them the gifts and graces which God has placed there, and do not receive these from them as from those who have received them from God, but to the contrary they despise and scorn both them and God their Author. For He has said: "He that heareth you heareth Me, and he that despiseth you despiseth Me" (Matt. 10:40; Luke 10:16). And, speaking of the power and authority of the magistrates to whom He has given the power of life and death and to whom He wills that every man be subject, He declared that whoever resists such a power resists God, not man (Rom. 13:2).

And, therefore, when God imparted His name to such persons because they represented His image, by this He shows us what obedience we owe them and that we must obey them out of our love for Him and must remember from whom they receive this authority and with whom we have to deal—that is, with Him whose name they bear, and not mortal men. Therefore those who are under their charge must keep themselves under bridle and under obedience and humility, knowing that they will have God as an adversary (just as He showed in the punishment of Korah, Dathan, Abiram, and their accomplices) if they rebel against their authorities as they rebelled against Moses and Aaron (Num. 16:1-35).

Yet neither are they guiltless if, in rendering the authorities the honor which is their due, they honor man more than God who wills to be honored in them.

TIMOTHY: This is very good advice.

OTHER WARNINGS WHICH ARE GIVEN TO THOSE TO WHOM THE NAME OF GOD IS IMPARTED BY THIS TITLE, SO THAT THEY MIGHT KNOW HOW TO GUIDE AND LEAD IN THEIR OFFICE; AND THE EXCELLENCE AND BEAUTY OF THE HEBREW LANGUAGE IN THIS MANNER OF SPEAKING

DANIEL: Also, those who are raised to such an honor must also courageously and properly acquit themselves in their office without fear of any creature whatever. For, if they execute their office in good conscience, they can rest assured that they are in God's safekeeping and that He will supply them power, strength, and force by which all their enemies shall tremble before them (as we have an example of in the good kings and rulers and the true prophets and servants of God to whom He gave the charge of His people).

On the other hand, they must truly fear if they act otherwise. They can rest assured that God will bring great vengeance against them for the injury which has been committed against Him by using His name as a mask for the devil and by honoring Satan while reigning under God's title and by using this as a cloak for their tyranny, duplicity, and evildoing.

This is also why the false and strange gods who are not gods at all are called gods. It is very true that with this declaration Holy Scripture often adds the words "false," "strange," "new," "vain," and other similar titles in order that we might understand in what esteem we must hold them. But at the same time it also declares to us how great is the conceit of man and how execrable is the sin of idolatry. For what, I say not only conceit, but also presumption, impudence, and passion, could be greater in man than attempting to create gods? For this is utterly impossible in himself, and more impossible for man than the creation of heaven and earth and of all other creatures. But what more could the devil himself attempt who strove to create gods himself, instead of God the Creator of all who was Himself content with making creatures? For gods which are made cannot be gods. Furthermore, what greater crime could man commit than to deny that God is God and to change Him into another and to place others—even the very devil himself—in His place?

TIMOTHY: How can man do what is utterly impossible?

DANIEL: He tries to do it as best as he can, although he may not consciously do it when he ascribes to the creatures the honor due to God. And, because he raises the creature to this height as much as he is able—though he cannot do it and cannot make him god or make God cease to exist—the Spirit of God, seeking to quite clearly bring to light this error, darkness, and perversity of the heart and human understanding, has called the seed, birth, and fruit of this perverse heart (which are these false gods) by the name which would best suit them if they were worthy of the honor ascribed to them, as though He respected the evil desire and fantasy by which they were conceived and begotten. And, because they cannot be so, He gives them the titles which suit them in order to declare the folly, conceit, hypocrisy, madness, and passion which there exists.

FOURTEEN

Worship and Its Meaning

THE WORD "WORSHIP" AND ITS MEANING

TIMOTHY: I now truly understand the reason why this name of God is thus imparted to the creatures, and in what sense it must be taken, and in what manner we fashion for ourselves strange gods. What you said concerning the faith and trust that we must place in God seems to me to also apply to all the other three points which still remain to be expounded. For, if those to whom we ascribe the honor of God contained in this first point are false gods to us, I do not doubt that it shall be the same with the others. Therefore let's continue now by order, and tell me first what you understand by the name *worship* and how it can be distinguished from the faith and trust we just discussed.

DANIEL: Worship properly means "to show reverence." This can be performed in various ways: in either abasing or lowering the body, in humbling oneself, in kneeling or falling to the ground and lying prostrate, in bowing the head only, or in lowering the hand. All these actions and other similar ones by which we declare the honor and reverence we bear someone (particularly our superiors and those who are high in office and dignity) are included under this name worship.

TIMOTHY: I understand this well. But do you wish to say that God requires this same worship of us which lies in the external form? Seeing that He is Spirit and that He wills to be "worshiped in spirit and truth" according to the testimony of Jesus Christ, it seems to me that this manner of worship is hardly proper to Him at all, but to the contrary that He requires another worship even more excellent and more fitting to His nature and majesty, which it could not be if it were not spiritual (John 4:23).

DANIEL: You come now to the main point. It is certain that God is in no way content with such a physical worship if it is not also joined with the spiritual. But you must also understand that He does not disapprove of this when it is so joined with the spiritual that it proceeds from it and bears witness to it, just like the confession made with the mouth to salvation. For "out of the abundance of the heart the mouth speaketh," as a testimony of the faith which is within (Matt. 12:34). Furthermore, seeing that God has also truly created the body as well as the soul and that it is His temple, He also desires to be glorified in it and receive homage from it (1 Cor. 6:19).

TIMOTHY: Then in this case there will be two types of worship toward God: one physical and the other spiritual.

DANIEL: It is true, as long as the physical and external worship is no more than a fruit and testimony of the internal and spiritual and is not put into practice except to incite and induce man to the spiritual, and to praise God among men, in testifying of the spiritual by it. Thus true servants of God do not render this external testimony unless it is also in their heart in truth, as they testify. This is the reason why not only spiritual worship is included and understood in the word worship, but also all honor and divine service are many times meant by it.

IN WHAT SENSE AND IN WHAT MEANING WORSHIP IS TAKEN WHEN IT IS A MATTER OF THE SERVICE OF GOD; AND THE DIFFERENCE BETWEEN IT AND THE FAITH AND TRUST THAT WE MUST HAVE IN HIM; AND TRUE FAITH, AND ITS NATURE; AND THE TRUE KNOWLEDGE OF GOD

TIMOTHY: Seeing that we agree on this point, tell me now what exactly you understand by this worship and how you wish to distinguish it from the faith and trust in God which we already discussed.

DANIEL: I here take *worship* for an homage which man renders to God by a true acknowledgement, humility, and submission of heart to Him, which he also declares by external signs when necessary, and by these recognizes and confesses God to be his Creator and the Creator of all things and to be just as we have already said concerning the faith and trust that He requires of us, recognizing and learning to know Him, and understanding and laying hold of Him.

TIMOTHY: I do not yet quite grasp the difference you place between the faith and trust we already discussed and this worship. To the contrary, it seems that all you say now of worship applies exactly to what was already said of faith and trust.

DANIEL: Let me then show you this difference a little more clearly. I place almost as much difference between trust and worship as we could place between knowledge and acknowledgement. For there is no acknowledgement which is not preceded by knowledge. For how can I acknowledge someone as my ruler whom I do not know to be my ruler? Thus I must first understand that he is my ruler and then, having understood, I must receive him as such. Then I can submit to and acknowledge him as my ruler by rendering him the homage which is due him. Now, when this is applied to God, man must first "believe that He is, and that He is a rewarder of them that diligently seek Him" (Heb. 11:6).

TIMOTHY: And how do we arrive at this knowledge?

DANIEL: By the hearing of the Word of God, from which faith proceeds, so that this knowledge is like a part, the beginning, and the first foundation of faith. And therefore this knowledge, if it is true, must be joined with a true trust in Him who is the object of our trust. The Holy Scripture often includes both these two things under the name of faith, referring to the whole by naming one of its parts. Therefore Paul said: "For whosoever shall call upon the name of the Lord shall be saved. How then shall they call on Him in whom they have not believed? and how shall they believe in Him of whom they have not heard? and how shall they hear without a preacher?" He then concludes: "So then faith cometh by hearing, and hearing by the word of God" (Rom. 10:13-14, 17; Joel 2:32; Acts 2:21).

Thus, when God is set forth to us in His Word and the Spirit of God works in our hearts by it, He works two things together: He makes God known to us in such a way that we are able to know Him, and also at the same time He teaches us to place our trust in Him. When these two things are joined together, then faith is true and complete. And, as much as these two things are within us to a greater or lesser degree, likewise faith is also either more or less perfect. Therefore we always have need of increasing in both of these things.

IMPERFECT AND FALSE FAITH; AND THE REASON WHY FAITH AND THE KNOWLEDGE OF GOD ARE TAKEN FOR EACH OTHER

TIMOTHY: And if it happens that one of these is lacking within us, can faith still be true faith?

DANIEL: No, but it is false and counterfeit, in no way possessing within itself what its name declares. For to what purpose serves the knowledge that we should have of God if it does not teach us to confide in Him and honor Him? How does this differ from the faith which the demons have, which is the reason why they "tremble" and fear, as James testifies (Jam. 2:19), but not as they ought? Because this false faith is without trust in God, they tremble for fear of His majesty instead of being assured by this, as are the good angels. Such is the faith of all those who misuse the knowledge of God like the demons do.

Also, the trust which lacks true knowledge of God cannot be true and certain, but on the contrary it is instead a whim and fancy of the human mind. For what trust can be placed in something which is not known and of which there exists no certain knowledge? For, where there is no certain knowledge, there can never be certain assurance except by opinion, conjecture, and assumption, which are never certain but to the contrary are always joined with doubt. Therefore the conscience can never be assured by them.

Therefore the *knowledge of God* is sometimes taken in the Holy Scriptures for *faith in God,* and *knowledge* for *belief,* as in this passage: "And this is life eternal, that they might know Thee the only true God, and Jesus Christ, whom Thou hast sent" (John 17:3). If to know God by Jesus Christ is life eternal and to believe on Jesus Christ in Him is likewise eternal life, it is then the same thing, at least in this passage.

Or, if we prefer, we might say that one of the parts is taken for the whole because one cannot be separated from the other in true faith. For there is only one way to arrive at this eternal life. Therefore, as often as this knowledge and understanding is divine rather than human and is only learned through the Holy Spirit alone and is joined with the trust we have spoken of, then Holy Scripture calls it *faith.*

Thus any faith and trust which is without this true knowledge is a false faith, which possesses no more than the appearance of faith. Such is the faith of the superstitious and idolatrous who possess zeal without knowledge and have some desire to serve God without being ruled by the knowledge of His Word. Thus we would do well to diligently note the confession that Peter made of Jesus Christ, saying: "We believe and are sure that Thou art that Christ, the Son of the living God" (John 6:69). He joins these two together, *belief* and *knowledge,* because the one proceeds from the other and because the two are joined together in true faith, which is by no means merely opinion without certain knowledge, or knowledge alone without trust and assurance.

FIFTEEN

Faith and Its Fruits

HOW FAITH BEGETS WORSHIP OF GOD; AND HOW CALLING ON HIM AND GIVING HIM THANKS AND THE OBEDIENCE WHICH IS DUE HIM ARE TYPES OF WORSHIP

TIMOTHY: It is required then, according to what you say, to possess both in true faith.

DANIEL: It is at least required that there be a true beginning. For we must never boast that we possess faith in its entirety and perfection while we are yet clothed in this flesh, but to the contrary we must always pray with the apostles and with the father of the boy with the unclean spirit: "Increase our faith" and: "Help Thou mine unbelief" (Luke 17:5; Mark 9:24).

And why is it that it always remains imperfect in us except that this knowledge and trust, without which it cannot be faith, are never wholly and perfectly in us during this life? But if we have the beginning, God, who has already given us what we have, will also complete the rest, as much as is required for our salvation.

And then, when the heart of man is thus prepared by true faith, this faith which bears the knowledge of God and trust in Him immediately gives birth to this worship of which we speak, which leads man to recognize His greatness and to bear Him reverence and to wholly submit to Him, and to humble himself, willingly taking all that he has and surrendering all to Him, worshiping His secret and unsearchable judgments and councils, though he cannot understand the reasons and causes.

It also induces him to render Him the homage which carries the acknowledgement of the honor due to Him alone by which He is set apart from every creature and honored above all things, as a sovereign ruler by his subjects.

Seeing that it is so, the true submission of the conscience to Him must not be lacking (which is also one of the main points pertaining to worship), by which we acknowledge that He is Lord of our consciences and that we have no other to whom they must be subject, and that we must make conscience of nothing except what we have in His Law and which concerns His majesty. Then from this same source follow invocation (or calling upon His name), thanksgiving, and obedience, which are due to God as expressions and declarations of this worship.

HOW THE PARTS PERTAINING TO THE WORSHIP OF GOD ARE OFTEN TAKEN FOR THE WHOLE AND PERFECT WORSHIP OF GOD—INDEED, EVEN THE EXTERNAL SIGNS THEMSELVES; AND WHY THIS IS DONE

TIMOTHY: From what I can understand, all these things are so linked and joined together that one cannot truly exist without the other, but to the contrary they are dependent on one another and are the fruits by which they reveal themselves.

DANIEL: It is true. And therefore it often happens (as was already mentioned) that one of these things is taken for all the others which are joined to it and for all the honor and worship which is due to God in the same way that in the Holy Scriptures the name of the external signs is often taken not only for the sign but also for that which it signifies. For, as God never deceives—either in word, promise, or sign—but to the contrary always gives the truth which He promises and declares, so also the believer is never false either in his words or works, but to the contrary he possesses such a heart toward God as he declares by his outward actions.

Therefore when our Lord Jesus Christ desired to contain all the Law in a summary, He reduced all under the love of God and one's neighbor (Matt. 22:36:40). For, just as the love of God cannot exist without love for one's neighbor, so also true love for God cannot exist without all the things we have already discussed. For, as it is commonly said: "We must know before we love, and trust whom we love." And then, being joined to Him by such a love, we have no difficulty in doing for Him all that we know is pleasing to Him. And therefore as soon as we have truly known God, we love Him, trust in Him, and then worship Him and submit our consciences to Him and call upon Him in all our needs, and give Him thanks for the blessings we receive from Him, and seek to be fully obedient to His will.

CALLING UPON THE NAME OF GOD; AND THANKSGIVING; AND THE DISTINCTION TO BE MADE IN GOOD WORKS

TIMOTHY: You thus understand by *invocation* or *calling upon Him* the appeal which the creature has to his Creator in all his needs. And, by *thanksgiving*, you mean the praises which man renders to God for the blessings he has received and the witness that he renders Him both by his words and works.

DANIEL: It is so.

TIMOTHY: We could thus include all sorts of entreaties and prayers and all the good works done by the faithful (and particularly the celebration of the sacraments ordained by God) under these names of *invocation* and *thanksgiving*, and as being different types of worship.

DANIEL: There is no great danger in taking it thus. But, in order to remove the confusion which might be created by joining all these things together, it would be better to distinguish them in order that we might more easily understand them:

Though all our good works are witnesses of the love we bear to God and the acknowledgement we make of His blessings, yet we prefer to confine under the name of *obedience* those works which chiefly concern the second Table of the Law and one's neighbor.

For the other commandments, we use the names *worship, invocation,* and *thanksgiving,* under which we can more easily reduce those which deal with the first Table and which have a particular consideration for the person of God alone.

TIMOTHY: Do you then mean that all these things must be returned to God alone just like trust, worship, and the submission of conscience which we already discussed, and that to ascribe them to another would be to create false gods?

DANIEL: Yes. And all who worship men in this way show great dishonor to God, for they ascribe to the creatures the honor which is due to Him. They also greatly abuse Him when they do not render Him what they owe Him, and who scorn His sacraments and ordinances. For it isn't enough to simply not render to the creature the honor which belongs to Him. But, while guarding against committing such an outrage against Him, we must also take care to render to Him the honor which is His due and not to live without God, as many do who care for neither God nor saint. But we must consider what is said in the preface to this Law: "I am the LORD thy God."

TIMOTHY: You touch now upon a point which is well worthy of notice. For there are many on earth today who are by no means idolaters (in the sense that they worship graven images), but are even worse; and it is truly difficult to judge which god they have. They have so great a fear of making false gods that they have none at all, but to the contrary have an even wickeder opinion of God than the Epicureans. Or, if they have some impression of Him, they imagine Him to be such as the Epicureans believe, denying His providence and denying Him to be the Creator and Judge of men.

DANIEL: It is quite true that there are such people as you say. Would that it pleased God that their number were not so great!

We might well add to these a heap of unbelieving scholars who, though they do not openly deny these things, yet they have come to no certain conclusion on them but remain forever in doubt, and they teach and affirm that we cannot know these things for certain. There are some among these who say that the Holy Scriptures also cannot be understood. They seek to lead men astray by telling them that they must await some new revelation from heaven, as though we were unable to know and understand with certainty the things which are already so clearly revealed in His Word.

TIMOTHY: These are most dangerous sects.

THE JUDGMENT OF GOD AGAINST THE EPICUREANS, ATHEISTS, AND UNBELIEVING SCHOLARS; AND HOW THOSE WHO SEEK TO BE WITHOUT GOD CANNOT WHOLLY EFFACE ALL KNOWLEDGE AND AWARENESS OF HIM FROM THEIR HEART AND MIND

DANIEL: It is no surprise that so many miserable people fall into such opinions that are not only more than beastly but more than diabolical. For, seeing that there are such today who in this most clear and full light of the Gospel of Jesus Christ so miserably abuse the truth which has been revealed and the knowledge which has been given them, and who prefer darkness rather than light and regard the justice of God as injustice rather than give to God the glory which pertains to Him, should we marvel if God gives such people over to a reprobate mind and if He removes their sense and understanding so that they become more beastly than the brute beasts? For this is the penalty with which, according to Paul, God is accustomed to punish such persons (Rom. 1:28).

And indeed, such wretches are not worthy of knowing the true God and of sensing the joy and consolation which the true knowledge of Him brings with it. They are not worthy to have God as their God, for He would be so dishonored to be the God of such pigs in the same way as He is the God of believers, and to be their God in any other way than He is the God of either the brute beasts or the devils and reprobates.

And, because these beastly errors are so far beyond the pale of reason that human reason itself can condemn many of them by its own natural judgment, God reveals to us by these most horrible creatures in what detestation we ought to hold human presumption and arrogance which not only imagines and invents but also dares to maintain and defend such strange and monstrous opinions of God. By this He quite openly displays His wrath and ire against such arrogant and presumptuous men. Yet, though such men desire to live without God, they cannot avoid having one and cannot avoid creating false gods for themselves just as the others do, no matter what they are, for they make false gods of themselves, seeing that they ascribe to themselves what they owe to God. This is why Paul, in speaking of false prophets, says that their "god is their belly" (Phil. 3:19). And consequently they must come to the same end as the other idolaters and they must also receive the devil—who blinds their eyes and understanding—as their god.

THOSE WHO CREATE FALSE GODS BY FALSE RELIGIONS AND HERESIES

TIMOTHY: I now understand all these things very clearly. What more do we have to discuss on this matter?

DANIEL: We can now better explain and understand at least what sort of gods the pagans and the Jews, Muslims, Papists, and heretics have who dishonor God by ascribing to the creature the honor which is due to Him alone. For, seeing that they do not in the least know the true God who gave this commandment as He revealed Himself in His Word (which alone is the Word of Truth), it is certain that all the opinions and imaginations which they have of God, by which they make Him something other than He is set forth to us in the Holy Scriptures, are just so many false gods that they fashion in their hearts. But we shall put this off till another time, and pursue the three other points which we must still explain, following the division we made at the beginning of the matters to deal with in this commandment.

TIMOTHY: This will be good.

SIXTEEN

The Wording of the First Commandment

WHY GOD SPEAKS IN HIS LAW IN A SINGULAR NUMBER AND NOT PLURAL; AND IN THE SECOND PERSON; AND IN A NEGATIVE RATHER THAN A POSITIVE MANNER

DANIEL: We must now explain the reason why God speaks in the singular and second person as if He were addressing someone in particular who was present there and not all generally in the third person, and why He has set this commandment down in a negative sense rather than using a positive manner of speaking.

TIMOTHY: I would truly like to know this also.

DANIEL: The fact that God speaks in the singular and in the second person, as though speaking to one person only who was there present, declares that each one of us must receive this commandment not as something which concerns us only in general but as something which is particularly addressed to us, as if we saw and heard God here speaking to each of us by name, face to face. For, though something spoken in general concerns us all, yet it does not press us so closely as when someone addresses us directly and when someone specifically informs us that what is spoken is spoken particularly for us.

And therefore God speaks to us as if we were there present, particularly addressing Himself to each of us one after the other, in order that we might understand that it is we whom

He is after and with whom He is dealing, and that we must not in any way think we can slip away in the anonymity of the crowd and hide ourselves among the multitude if we do otherwise than what He commands, as if He would not notice.

He also employs the negative (in forbidding something) because it carries with it more than the positive and more than a simple commandment. For, when He says: "Thou shalt have no other gods before Me," He sets forth three things all at the same time:

The first is that we must have a God, and man must not exist without acknowledging one.

Second, it is He who must be taken and acknowledged as such. And, also, there is a hidden antithesis and opposition couched within this negative manner of speaking, if we recall what He said in the preface: "I am the Lord thy God." He desires to declare to us by this that it is He who must be received as God.

Thirdly, it is not sufficient for us to acknowledge and receive Him as God, but we must also receive Him alone as such, without adding another to Him. For we cannot add another without denying that He is God, seeing that there must necessarily be either no gods at all or only one alone (as we have already shown by good reasons).

Now, if He had said: "Thou shalt take Me as thy God," it would have appeared that there were many gods and that it was permissible to add others and render to them their due honor and that it was sufficient for Him to have His part and to be a companion of the others and to be served, just as it is written in the Holy Scriptures that the Samaritans served Him after they were placed in Samaria by the kings of Assyria, and just as all the idolaters served Him (2 Kings 17:28-33). For, though they made many false gods, yet they all prided themselves in the fact that they not only worshiped the true God but that they also gave Him the best place among all the others. But when He says: "Thou shalt have no other," He puts a complete end to all these thoughts, excuses, and good appearances of the idolaters and an end to all idolatry and superstition, declaring that whoever does not take Him as his God alone cannot have Him as his God at all.

WHY GOD EXPRESSLY MENTIONS HIS PRESENCE AMONG THE TRANSGRESSORS OF THIS COMMANDMENT; AND WHAT IT IS TO HAVE FALSE GODS BEFORE HIM; AND HOW NOTHING CAN BE HIDDEN FROM HIM

TIMOTHY: This is a point well worthy of note and one which is little understood by men. For, if it were well understood, all idolatry and all false religion would instantly cease.

I believe that we have now clearly settled the main points to note in this commandment, and particularly those which were dealt with in the division which you made.

DANIEL: Nothing further remains, in my opinion, except to explain the reason why God, after forbidding us to have strange gods, added these words here: "before Me," or, if you prefer it another way: "in My presence" or "before My face." This is a statement which must be closely examined in order to make us more attentive to the observance of this commandment.

TIMOTHY: Why is this?

DANIEL: Because, firstly, He declares to us by these words that we must not do, say, or think anything against this commandment and against all His will, and that if we have the least regard for false gods or the least thought of apostasy, He will see it and He Himself will be a Witness and Judge against us for it.

This crime of apostasy and idolatry is often concealed before men, either because man practices it secretly in his heart or because he cunningly disguises it by his ruses and hypocrisies and by the ornaments with which he decorates it. Therefore God truly desired to declare by these words that man cannot begin to know how to be so secret or how to so well disguise, conceal, and hide his idolatry and apostasy that God cannot see it clearly and that He cannot easily bring it to light.

Secondly, He also desired to suppress by this means the audacity and wickedness of the human heart and to reveal its insanity and rage and to declare what offense man shows Him when he violates this commandment. For man declares by this that he does not believe that God can see and know him as He does see and know, and that he does not receive Him as God.

Or, if he does believe that God can see and know him, he shows by this that he fears Him very little indeed and that he has very little concern for Him, or that he takes express pleasure in angering Him by paying Him such a dishonor before His very face, as if an adulteress had publicly prostituted herself with her lovers in contempt of her husband and before his very eyes.

TIMOTHY: This would be a truly villainous dishonor. Therefore this admonition is quite necessary for us. For in this case we must not toy or play with God, but must walk with Him in all simplicity of heart and true frankness as those who know that they walk exposed and in public and that they deal with a Lord who sees as clearly by night as by day, who knows not only all our works and words, but also all our thoughts and the deepest secrets of our hearts, and to whom we must render an account.

DANIEL: You conclude quite well. And therefore let us remember the preface which the Lord declared before giving His commandments. Let us diligently remember what a God He is, what authority He has over us, what blessings we have received from Him, and how He is to be feared and loved.

Let us likewise remember to take Him alone as our God and to render Him the honor which is His due—that is, faith, worship, invocation, thanksgiving, the subjection of our consciences, and the obedience He requires of us.

And let us beware of fashioning for ourselves false gods in the manner we have discussed. And let us not allow ourselves to be seduced either by earthly benefits or by the beautiful appearances by which idolaters are accustomed to disguise their superstitions and idolatries. But let us wholly dedicate and consecrate ourselves to God and His service.

TIMOTHY: That is very sensible.

SEVENTEEN

No Other God

A Sermon by John Calvin

"The Lord talked with you face to face in the mount out of the midst of the fire, (I stood between the Lord and you at that time, to shew you the word of the Lord: for ye were afraid by reason of the fire, and went not up into the mount;) saying, I am the Lord thy God, which brought thee out of the land of Egypt, from the house of bondage. Thou shalt have none other gods before Me."
— Deuteronomy 5:4-7

We've already seen how Moses took great pains to explain to the people the majesty found within God's Word in order that they might receive it with all reverence. For, though men truly declare that they are quite willing to serve God (for even nature drives them to this), yet they don't desire to submit themselves to His Word despite the fact that this is the true test that proves whether we are obedient to God or not. But by this the rebelliousness of the world is clearly revealed. And, even though they may say that God's Word should be received without question, yet you can scarcely find one among a hundred who truly and earnestly humbles himself and yields to the authority of His Word as he ought to. And why is this? It's because we don't comprehend the majesty of God which is revealed within it.

Thus you see why Moses had such good reason to declare so many times previously that God's Word must be viewed by us with such majesty that all creatures ought to tremble at it.

And now again he adds another confirmation of this, saying: "The Lord talked with you face to face in the mount out of the midst of the fire" (Deut. 5:4). This is the same as if he had said: "You now have no reason at all to doubt whether the doctrine that I deliver to you is from God or from men. You see that it is clear and obvious enough—and more than enough, for God has revealed Himself to you by visible and very evident signs, so much so that you can't deny that it's He who has spoken to you." Now we see Moses' meaning.

But, before we go any further, the question might be raised: how can it be said that God spoke face to face, seeing that men can't comprehend His infinite glory? And with what eye can we behold the essence of God? We are so weak-sighted that if God only cast a very little beam of His glory on us we would immediately be completely blinded and confounded.

Also, we know that it's written that we can't see God face to face until we are renewed, which won't be until the last day. For, just as Paul says, we now only see as through a glass, and in part, and darkly (1 Cor. 13:12; 15:51-52).

He also says in another place that the Gospel now reveals God's glory to us in such a way that we can behold Him in it. But under the Law this was obscured and a veil hung over it which hindered the fathers from knowing God in the same way and so intimately as we do today (2 Cor. 3:15-18).

But yet there is no contradiction between these Scriptures. For, when the Law is compared with the Gospel, we see clearly that what Paul says here is true. For God didn't reveal Himself so intimately at that time as He does to us through our Lord Jesus Christ, who is His express image (Heb. 1:2-3; Col. 1:15; 2:3). Therefore in our day the great treasures of God's wisdom are laid forth so openly that we understand how God calls us to the kingdom of heaven and how He receives us as His children and heirs (Eph. 1:5-14; 1 Thess. 2:12). This wasn't so in the time of the Law.

And yet, even though we possess such a deep and intimate knowledge today, yet it's still true that even with all our knowledge we only see in part. Why is this? It's because we aren't yet made partakers of God's glory and therefore we can't approach Him, but He must instead be pleased to reveal Himself to us according to our ignorance and weakness. Even though God has appeared to men even from the beginning of the world, yet He has never shown Himself in His actual being but only in a way that men were able to endure. Therefore we must always return to this point, that God was neither known to the fathers nor does He appear to us in our day in His essence. But He reveals Himself to us as much as He is pleased to stoop down to make us perceive His presence according to our ability.

Yet it certainly wasn't without reason that Moses says here: "The Lord talked with you face to face" (Deut. 5:4). He means by this that the people weren't left with only some vague or indistinct impression or conjecture of Him in such a way that they could doubt Him or only conceive some uncertain opinion of Him. But, to the contrary, they had an infallible proof, so much so that they might conclude: "Here is God who has so revealed Himself to us that our faith must never be uncertain anymore. Neither should the instruction which is set forth to us in His name ever be disputed or called into question or be debated whether it's good for us to receive it or not. Why is this? It's because God has given us a certain sign which can't deceive us or leave us in any doubt that it proceeded from Him." Thus we now see Moses' meaning.

We have a good lesson to learn in this: even if God didn't reveal Himself in such a stately manner as we might have desired Him to, yet we must assure ourselves that His doing so is for our good and wellbeing. For, if we consider our own infirmity, this will abase the audacity which our nature is always prone to. For we never cease to inquire into God's secrets. Why is this? It's because we don't recognize our own inability. Therefore let us magnify the goodness of our God because it pleased Him to have a regard for us and our lowliness and ignorance and to conceal His glory from us lest we should be overwhelmed by it. For, as I said before, we couldn't bear it because of our frailty.

And from this we must understand that there is no excuse for us if we refuse to yield to God His due honor when He has given us such a clear token of His presence.

Therefore we mustn't expect God to come to us in His inestimable glory or that the heavens should be rent asunder and all the angels of paradise should appear to us. But, when our Lord has shown us that it is He who speaks, let that be enough for us, and let us humble ourselves at once. For, if we are slothful in this case, we will be condemned for turning our backs on Him when He showed His face to us. Indeed, it's said to us in another place that no one can see God's face without perishing (Ex. 33:20). So unable are we to behold Him that, even when He showed himself to Moses in such an intimate way, just as a man speaks with his friend, yet even so it's said that he saw nothing more than His back parts (Ex. 33:11, 20, 23).

This is to continuously show us that we must never presume to approach God too closely as long as we are in this flesh. We mustn't attempt to raise ourselves so high. For, if the angels themselves, under the shape of seraphim, hide their eyes when God shows Himself, what should we do who can only crawl here on earth? (Isa. 6:2.)

But, even though this is the case, yet God will condemn us for our ungratefulness if we have no desire to behold His face and if the tokens of His presence which He has revealed to us aren't enough for us. Above all, therefore, let us bear this in mind: we must submit ourselves both to the Law as well as to the Gospel, for it is here that God principally wills to reveal Himself to men in order that they might worship Him, receiving with childlike trust everything that proceeds from His mouth.

How then should we apply this saying of Moses? In this way: whenever the Scripture is set before us—either while it's being preached and expounded to us or when we read it ourselves—this preface to the Law must serve to humble us in order that we might exalt God with all reverence and that we might not dare to reply against this Word but rather tremble before it, just as the prophet Isaiah writes (Isa. 66:2, 5). For everything that is contained in the Holy Scriptures is so thoroughly revealed and proved to us that it may truly be said that God has talked with men—yes, and that He has even shown Himself to them in a visible way.

Next Moses adds: "I stood between the Lord and you at that time, to shew you the word of the Lord: for ye were afraid by reason of the fire, and went not up into the mount" (Deut. 5:5). By this Moses shows us that, though the Law was given by a mortal man, yet this ought not to diminish its authority. Why is this? Because the infirmity of the people required this; this was their sin.

This is a verse well worthy of note, for we are always seeking loopholes to slip through so that we can despise God's Word. It's true that we won't confess this openly, but yet each of us are so wickedly inclined that we think we're safe if we can find any excuse or justification for saying: "Ah, now, I don't know for sure whether this is truly God's Word or not. I can't tell whether it applies to me or not. I don't know what conditions are attached to it."

Thus we see how everyone continually labors to exempt themselves from obedience to God's Word. It's a very common excuse to say: "Yes, certainly God ought to be obeyed, but yet those who preach His Word are only men just like ourselves. And should we listen to and obey their teaching as though these men had appeared to us from heaven?" Many people truly believe that this excuse is sufficient, but they are still rebels against God by utterly absolving themselves from submitting to Him and His Word in any way at all.

But we have an answer here which will cut short all these excuses: when God sends His Word by the hand of men, He does so out of consideration for man's sin and infirmity. Yet He doesn't fail to give us some mark of His glory by which His Word is sufficiently recognized to be divine, so much so that if the matter is diligently considered, it's clear that God has thoroughly authenticated it. So then, it wasn't only written for the men of old that Moses spoke this, but this warning is also directed to us in order that we might know that, though men are appointed as messengers to preach God's Word to us, yet this in no way diminishes His Word's majesty and glory.

And, indeed, we misunderstand our own frailty when we

ask God to work miracles daily; nor indeed do we know what's good for us. For, concerning miracles, there have been enough of them worked already for the full authentication of the truth both of the Law and of the Gospel in order that we might fully believe them. Yet we are truly today in need of God sending us men like ourselves, to whom He has given the commission to teach us in His name and stead, as one who draws us to Him with all gentleness and lovingkindness.

Do we really think we are capable of bearing His presence if He appeared to us in His essence? Indeed, no! We would be utterly consumed. If God were to speak in His power, we know that (just as it's written) the rocks and mountains themselves would melt (Psa. 97:5; Isa. 64:1-3; Mic. 1:4). And could we, who are as feeble as anything could be, be able to withstand such power in such a way that it wouldn't thunder down upon us and destroy us?

Therefore let's truly note that when God ordained His Word to be preached to us and willed that we should have it in writing, by doing this He condescended to our weakness and dealt with us as if He Himself were a mortal man, in order that we might not be afraid to come to Him but might instead be drawn to Him with all gentleness.

Again, what great honors does He bestow on us by being pleased to choose men of no reputation among us to proclaim His person and to speak to us in His name? For what more could He give to the angels in heaven? Could He have given them a more honorable duty or calling? Seeing then that He condescends to set men in so noble and excellent a position as to proclaim His Word, by this He shows how great His goodness is towards us—that He loves us more than a father.

And by this He also tests our humility. For, if He instead thundered from heaven and appeared visibly to us, and if the angels came down to us to proclaim His Word, it would be no surprise if men believed in His Word. But when both great and small embrace the order that He has established in His Church (that is, when they obey His Word preached to them), this is a true witness of our faith.

Yet we must always return to the fact that God has sufficiently revealed Himself to men so that we have no reason to doubt His Word or to dispute about it to determine its origin. For we are quite certain of His will if we aren't too stubborn to refuse the signs He has given us. Thus you see what we must learn from this sentence of Moses when he says that the people dared not go up into the mountain because of the fear they had. And, though in these days we think that we wouldn't refuse God if He chose to speak directly to us, yet if we truly consider the matter we can see that this wouldn't benefit or profit us at all. Therefore let us understand that God's use of men's service in this way ought not to diminish the certainty of our faith.

It's next said that God taught the people, saying: "I am the LORD thy God, which brought thee out of the land of Egypt, from the house of bondage. Thou shalt have none other gods before Me" (Deut. 5:6-7).

Here, in order to hold the people of Israel in check, God tells them that the knowledge which they have of Him ought to keep them far from all idolatry. For it shouldn't be surprising that the heathen had idols and went wandering after their own errors and imaginations. We understand that it's man's nature to do this. It's a pity to see how much we are inclined to such vanity and folly. We needn't go to school to learn to be deceived, for every one of us is a professional at it. In short, we always leap forward into evil (especially when it's concealed under the disguise of something good) in such a way that, instead of serving God, we find nothing within us but corruption and idolatry. This is why the heathen possessed their various idols, for every man forged whatever he imagined out of his own brain; and in the meantime the living God was abandoned by all. And why was this? It's because He didn't show the same grace to the entire world as to reveal Himself to all. And thus men became beastly and savage for lack of instruction. Yet they were still without excuse, for they are always guilty before God. The other source of idolatry is ungratefulness and wickedness, when men knowingly and willingly forsake God. But, when the world had so degenerated (as I mentioned previously), the miserable heathen ran astray like blind men, for they had no light to show them the way of salvation.

Now here God charges the people of Israel with rebellion if they refuse to keep the law that He gave them. Why is this? "I am the Lord thy God." When He says "I am the Lord" He excludes all the gods that have ever been invented by men. It's the same as if He had said: "There is only one Godhead and it is found in Me. Therefore all who know Me and who yet turn to idols can't excuse themselves, but have willfully forsaken the living God."

And, because He adds that He is the God of this people, He shows that He had sufficiently revealed Himself. It's as if He said: "I've gathered you out of all other peoples. You see how all the others are wandering astray for lack of guidance and direction. But I have chosen you for My people and have given Myself to you.

"Seeing then that I am your God," He says, "keep yourselves for Me from now on, or else you will be less excusable than the heathen. If you go astray, your punishment will be double—yes, and a hundred times more grievous than theirs—because you will have betrayed the faith that you swore to Me and have broken the covenant that I made with you."

He further declares the favor that He had shown them, saying: "[I] brought thee out of the land of Egypt, from the house of bondage" (Deut. 5:7). By this He means that He had so bound the people to Himself that they couldn't forsake Him without meriting grave punishment. For, because they would have to forget the deliverance they had received from Him, their ungratefulness would be double. Seeing that they had been redeemed by the hand of God, it was necessary for them to give themselves entirely to the service of Him who was their Redeemer.

He deliberately calls Egypt "the house of bondage" in order to make the people thoroughly consider the troubles they had experienced there. For we see how they sighed and cried out when they were oppressed with such violence and tyranny as we read of in Exodus (Ex. 2:23). Yet they desired to return there again as soon as God had delivered them (Ex. 14:12; 17:3; Num. 14:3-4). How could they desire to return? It could only be because they had forgotten their oppression and because the devil had blinded their eyes so that they didn't esteem God's grace as it deserved. This is why Moses calls Egypt the house of bondage.

After this the commandment is added which says: "Thou shalt have none other gods before Me" or "before My face," for He alone ought to be acknowledged as their God (Deut. 5:7).

Now let's apply all this teaching to our own use.

First of all, because He says, "I am the LORD," let us learn to ponder this saying in such a way that, seeing that God's majesty has appeared to us, we never imagine or follow any other Godhead. For God can't tolerate any equal. If the sun darkens the light of all the stars, isn't it sensible that when God shows Himself all men should worship Him and that all glory which might have been visible previously should then be as though it were nonexistent? This is why it's said by the prophets that when the Lord reigns there will be no other light than His, so much so that even the sun will be dimmed and the moon will be turned into darkness (Isa. 13:10; 24:23; Eze. 32:7). This serves to show us that if we mix any of the imaginations of our own heads with God, we diminish the right that belongs to Him. For He can't bear to have any equal. Therefore this word "LORD" must drive all imaginations and inventions far from us in such a way that we dare not imagine anything at all. Let's simply be content to have only one God, and let Him suffice us.

This is why it's also said that all the idols of Egypt will fall when our Lord Jesus sets up His throne in the world (Isa. 19:1). Now this text applies to us. For, just like Moses said to the people of his time, "The LORD has appeared to you, and therefore you must drive away all idols from your midst," so now, seeing that God has revealed Himself to us in the person of His only Son, it's imperative that all idols should be cast down (1 Tim. 3:16). We know that the land of Egypt was full of and bursting with idols above all the rest of the world.

Now then, just as we also were previously plunged into

lies and darkness and had an infinite number of idols, all those things must melt and vanish away when God tells us that He is the Lord.

Also, when He calls Himself *our God,* He does this to reveal Himself to us so that we can know His majesty and glory in a loving way. For, if God only spoke of His eternal nature and being, we would for the most part be utterly dismayed. It's true that this is enough to condemn all our follies. Yet, for all that, we still couldn't be properly instructed by this for our own use and profit.

Therefore, after God here revealed that He alone is to be worshipped and honored, He also spoke to us in a gentle and tender manner so that we might recognize Him as our Father and Master and might know that He wills to make a covenant with us in order that we might be joined to Him. This is what is meant by the title ascribed to Him in this text. It's the same as if He had said, "I don't only come as the Sovereign Lord to terrify you, but I am also your God. I have chosen you for Myself and I intend to have you for My inheritance" (*see* Deut. 4:20).

Now then, we see how God authorizes His Law so that we might receive it with all reverence, fear, and humility. And yet we also see that He condescends to make it sweet to our taste in order that we might taste it and take pleasure in submitting ourselves to it and in allowing ourselves to be ruled by the teaching contained within it.

Thus, in summary, we are left without excuse if we fail to honor our God today by renouncing all superstitions and all things contrary to His service. Why? Because the titles which He here attributes to Himself ought to draw us to Him. When He speaks of His sovereignty over us and says that He is our God, that ought to make us taste His fatherly goodness. And both of them are contained here.

We see then that nothing more remains for us to do except to listen to and obey the things told us in God's Law and to bind ourselves fully to it. This is the reason why He reproached the people of Israel, because they neither loved Him nor feared Him. "If then I be a father," He asks by the prophet Malachi, "where is Mine honour? and if I be a master, where is My fear?" (Mal. 1:6.) Where is our love for Him? Malachi was doubtless thinking of what Moses here recorded. For, when God names Himself the Lord, He does so in order that we should yield Him the reverence that is due Him. And, because He names Himself the God of that people, He intends to win them by friendliness and to show them that, because He had chosen them, they had good reason to place themselves entirely in His hands.

Now, if these things were true under the law, how much more are they true for us today? For, though God condescended to be as it were humbled in the person of His only Son, yet He still retained His glory, and Christ's incarnation was no diminution of the majesty here mentioned (Phil. 2:7). The abasement of our Lord Jesus Christ was an infallible evidence of the mercy of our God, but yet it most certainly shouldn't lead us to despise Him. For it was God's will to draw us to His infinite glory by this means in order that we should worship Him, seeing that He came down to us in that way.

Therefore He can justly reproach us nowadays and declare that we are utterly inexcusable if we refuse to both fear and love Him. For He has shown Himself to be both our God and our Master. Why then do we show no fear in rejecting His commandments? Are we instead so hardhearted at His threatening that we despise them and continue on in our evil deeds and make a mockery of His Law even when He shows Himself to be our Judge and calls us to a reckoning? Where is the reverence that we owe to our God? For, if He were a mortal creature, we would stand in more dread of Him than we do of the living God who has all authority over us.

Also, it isn't enough for us to fear God in a servile manner as if by constraint; but our fear must be joined with love. This is the reason why He calls Himself our Father. And we should also note that, when He declared Himself to be the God of Israel, He also declares Himself to be our Savior as well under this figure of speech. "Art thou not from everlasting, O Lord my God, mine Holy One?" asks the prophet Habakkuk; "We shall not die" (Hab. 1:12). Thus let us truly bear these titles in mind, for they belong to us and they ought to serve for our instruction in these days when the majesty of God has appeared in our Lord Jesus Christ (1 Tim. 3:16).

And here we must also notice what He adds concerning the favor that He showed to His people. "I have brought thee out of the land of Egypt" He says. Truly by this God meant to bind the people of Israel to Himself in a most special way above all other nations. (This is why He expressly mentions the deliverance that He brought to them.) So also, when God speaks, we must call to mind all the blessings by which He has bound us to Himself, which are infinite and inestimable. We must taste them as much as we can and must apply all our understanding to them. And, as much as we see ourselves falling short of this, we must strive all the harder to know at least as much of them as might teach us to fear and love our God.

Does God then speak? We must first consider that it is He who has created and fashioned us; therefore we are His. Here indeed is a special blessing already! Even if He had done no more for us than to establish us in this world and to preserve us in it, could we ever repay Him as we ought to, even if each of us endeavored to serve Him to the uttermost of our ability?

And yet what should our response be when we even further behold the records of His love which He gives us both from heaven and on earth, seeing that He created the world for our sakes and ordained and appointed all things for our use; and that He printed His image upon us and made us immortal; and that He has prepared a better inheritance for us than this fleeting life? (Gen. 1:26-28; Psa. 8:4-8; Heb. 9:15; 11:16; 1 Pet. 1:4.) When we see all these things, wouldn't we be the most stupid things alive if we weren't enraptured by His love and filled with an ardent desire to worship our God and to vow and dedicate ourselves entirely to Him?

But besides this we must consider all the good that God has shown to each of us, both in general and in particular, and then we must confess with David: "Many, O LORD my God, are Thy wonderful works which Thou hast done, and Thy thoughts which are to us-ward: they cannot be reckoned up in order unto

Thee: if I would declare and speak of them, they are more than can be numbered" (Psa. 40:5, 12). His blessings are more in number that the hairs of our head. Again, when we've acknowledged how much we owe to our God even in general, let us also consider the blessings that each of us have personally received from God's hand.

And, just as it was formerly said to the people of Israel "I brought thee out of the land of Egypt," so let us consider what our Lord delivered us from when He condescended to adopt us into His household and Church. For we are Adam's children, cursed by nature, heirs of death, altogether sinful, and consequently are exceedingly loathsome to our God (Rom. 5:14; Eph. 2:3). Thus, though men may cherish themselves and boast of their own glory as much as they like, yet this is their lineage, this is their only claim to fame: they are Satan's slaves, they have a sinkhole of sin and corruption within them, and they have nothing but God's wrath and curse hanging over their heads (Eph. 2:12; 4:18; 2 Tim. 2:26). And, in short, they've been banned from the kingdom of heaven and are delivered up to all misery and woe.

But our Lord has delivered us from these things by the hand of His Son (Acts 26:18). He hasn't sent us a Moses like He did to the people of old—but instead He didn't spare His only Son but delivered Him up to death for us (Rom. 8:32; 1 Pet. 1:19). Seeing then that we have been ransomed with so costly and inestimable a price as the holy blood of the Son of God, shouldn't we completely and entirely give ourselves to Him?

Also, if Egypt was termed a house of bondage, I ask you what we should call it when the devil holds us in his bonds and under his tyranny so that we have no means to escape death but are shut out from all hope of salvation, and God is utterly against us? Seeing that we are delivered from all these things, isn't this a much more excellent deliverance than that which Moses here speaks of? Thus, instead of what was said to the people of old: "Your God brought you out of the land of Egypt," now it's said to us: "Ye are not your own," and we must not live to ourselves (Rom. 14:7-9; 1 Cor. 6:19; 7:20-24). We aren't our own. Believers mustn't give themselves liberty to do what they like or to live each after his own desire. Why? Because our Lord Jesus Christ died and is risen again to reign over both the living and the dead. Thus Jesus Christ has good reason to be the Lord of life and death, seeing that He didn't spare Himself when our redemption and salvation were accomplished.

And, besides the fact that the Son of God offered up Himself for our redemption, let's remember that today He makes us partakers of that blessing by means of the Gospel. For He gathers us to Himself with the intent that we should be a part His flock (Eph. 1:10-13). He is most certainly the spotless Lamb which takes away the sins of the world, and He has truly offered Himself up to reconcile men unto God (John 1:29; Rom. 5:10; 2 Cor. 5:19; 2 Tim. 1:9-10).

But yet for all that we see a great number of people that are let alone, against whom the gate is shut, and to whom God doesn't grant the grace to be enlightened by faith as we are. Therefore let's truly note that, seeing that the Gospel is preached to us and we have within it an assurance that the Son of God will make the redemption available to us which He accomplished once and for all and will cause us to enjoy the benefit of it, we must learn that our thanklessness and ingratitude will be much wickeder and more shameful if we don't strive to give ourselves to our God who has bound us to Himself in this way.

If unbelievers play the part of runaway horses and break all bounds in their superstitions and in the wickedness of their lives, it's because they have no bridle and because He hasn't reigned them in as He does with His own. We see the horrible confusion of this in the papacy; but yet there is no teaching there which might lead men back to God. Instead it only alienates and drives them from Him. And we see that the devil has obtained such a hold there that everything is full of deception and smoke and mirrors and that the living God is forsaken. This is why such a horrible confusion and chaos reigns there.

But, on our part, seeing that God has drawn us to Himself, could we ask for a tighter bond to fully unite us with Himself and to hold ourselves under obedience to the teaching set forth to us in His name? Therefore let's learn to cleave to our God in such a way that we renounce everything we might ever imagine out of our own head, and let's remember that it isn't our place to swerve one way or the other or to be tossed to and fro in any way. But let us instead assure ourselves that there is but one God alone who chooses to possess us—yes, and who will possess us in such a way that His honor won't be taken from Him and bestowed on the creatures. It's He who watches over us. Thus let's acknowledge that it is He alone on whom we must call and to whose grace we must flee for refuge (Psa. 116:8-9).

And, finally, just as He wills to receive and accept us as members of His household, let us ever walk as in His presence and in His sight. Indeed, let this be done in such a way that we worship Him as our only God, not only with ceremonies and outward profession, but also in the worship of our hearts, for we know that His worship is spiritual (John 4:24).

In summary, we must let Him possess both our bodies and our souls in order that He might be thoroughly glorified in all (Rom. 12:1; 1 Pet. 1:22).

Now let us kneel in the presence of our good God with acknowledgement of our sins, praying Him to make us better recognize them, that it might lead us to true repentance and that we might mortify them more and more so that our wicked lusts might be cut off and we might be utterly given to fear and honor Him. And, because we can't serve Him perfectly as He deserves as long as we are burdened with the infirmities of our flesh, may it please Him to uphold us until He has clothed us with His own righteousness.

www.ingramcontent.com/pod-product-compliance
Ingram Content Group UK Ltd.
Pitfield, Milton Keynes, MK11 3LW, UK
UKHW041852190726
13854UKWH00002B/853

9 798609 793515